FUNDAMENTAL ISSUES IN PRESENT-DAY CHINA

Deng Xiaoping

Translated by
The Bureau for the Compilation and Translation of Works of Marx, Engels, Lenin and Stalin Under the Central Committee of the Communist Party of China

FOREIGN LANGUAGES PRESS BEIJING

First Edition 1987

Hard Cover: ISBN 0-8351-2103-8 ISBN 7-119-00344-5
Paperback: ISBN 0-8351-2106-2 ISBN 7-119-00345-3

Printed by the Foreign Languages Printing House
19 West Chegongzhuang Road, Beijing, China

Published by the Foreign Languages Press
24 Baiwanzhuang Road, Beijing, China

Distributed by China International Book Trading
Corporation (Guoji Shudian) P.O. Box 399, Beijing, China

Printed in the People's Republic of China

EDITORS' NOTE

In his opening speech at the Twelfth National Congress of the Chinese Communist Party, Comrade Deng Xiaoping analysed China's recent historical experience, focusing on one important idea—that we must integrate the universal truth of Marxism with the concrete realities of China, blaze a path of our own and build socialism with Chinese characteristics. This idea has become the general guiding principle for modernizing China. Since the Congress, Comrade Deng Xiaoping has further elaborated on it and elucidated many fundamental issues in present-day China relating to politics, the economy, ideology, science and technology, culture, education, foreign policy and so forth. The present volume is a collection of important talks and speeches he made on these matters between September 1982 and June 1987. The entire Chinese text was reviewed by the author himself.

Department for Research on Party
Literature, Central Committee of
the Communist Party of China

June, 1987

Deng Xiaoping talking with Chen Yun (left), Li Xiannian (second from right), and Zhao Ziyang (far right). (June 22, 1983)

Deng speaking at the National Conference of the Chinese Communist Party held on September 23, 1985.

With deputies to the Fifth Session of the Sixth National People's Congress. (April 1987)

Deng on the roof of the Shenzhen International Commerce Building, overlooking a new area under construction in Luohu. (January 24, 1984)

With Prime Minister Margaret Thatcher of the United Kingdom at the signing ceremony of the Sino-British Joint Declaration on the Question of Hongkong. (December 19, 1984)

Deng reviewing the three services of the PLA on October 1, 1984, the 35th anniversary of the founding of the People's Republic.

With Prime Minister Robert Mugabe
of Zimbabwe. (January 20, 1987)

Deng welcomed by a group of American friends, overseas Chinese residing in the U.S. and Chinese-Americans in Washington. (January 1979)

Laying the cornerstone for the Beijing National Laboratory in the suburbs of Beijing, which will house an electron-positron collider. The Laboratory will be part of the Institute of High Energy Physics, which is under the Chinese Academy of Sciences. (October 7, 1984)

At a banquet in honour of Todor Zhivkov (left), General Secretary of the Central Committee of the Bulgarian Communist Party and President of the State Council of Bulgaria. (May 7, 1987)

With Kaheita Okazaki, Advisor to the Japanese-Asian Exchange Association and Permanent Advisor to the Japan-China Economic Association. (August 30, 1985)

With a delegation of minority nationality youth from border regions visiting Beijing. (May 1, 1982)

CONTENTS

OPENING SPEECH AT THE TWELFTH NATIONAL CONGRESS OF THE COMMUNIST PARTY OF CHINA

September 1, 1982

Comrades,

I now declare the Twelfth National Congress of the Communist Party of China open.

There are three main items on our agenda: (1) to consider the report of the Eleventh Central Committee and decide on the Party's programme for opening up new prospects in all fields of socialist modernization; (2) to consider and adopt the new Constitution of the Communist Party of China; and (3) in accordance with the provisions of the new Party Constitution, to elect a new Central Committee, a Central Advisory Commission and a Central Commission for Discipline Inspection.

When these tasks have been accomplished, our Party will have clearer ideological guidelines for socialist modernization, our efforts to build the Party will conform more closely to the needs of the new historical period, and new cadres will be able to co-operate with old cadres and succeed them in the Party's highest organs which will thus provide even more vigorous and militant leadership.

A review of the Party's history will prove this Congress to be one of the most important since our Seventh National Congress.

The Seventh Congress, held in 1945 under Comrade Mao Zedong's chairmanship, was the most important in the period of democratic revolution after the founding of our Party. The delegates summed up the historical experience gained in the tortuous development of that revolution during the preceding quarter of a century, formulated a correct programme and correct tactics and overcame the wrong ideas inside the Party. They thus achieved a unity of understanding based on Marxism-Leninism and Mao Zedong Thought. As a result, the Party became more united than ever before. It was the Seventh Congress that laid the foundation for the nationwide victory in the new-democratic revolution.

The Eighth Congress of the Party in 1956 analysed the situation after the basic completion of the socialist transformation of private ownership of the means of production and presented the nation with the task of all-round socialist construction. Its line was correct. However, because the Party was still inadequately prepared ideologically for all-round socialist construction, that line and the many correct views put forward at the Congress were not fully implemented. After the Eighth Congress, we achieved many successes in socialist construction, but we also suffered serious setbacks.

The present Congress is being held in circumstances vastly different from those prevailing at the time of the Eighth Congress. Just as the quarter century of tortuous development of our democratic revolution before the Seventh Congress taught the Party the laws governing that revolution, so the quarter century of tortuous development of our socialist revolution and construction since the Eighth Congress has taught the Party other profound lessons. Since the Third Plenary Session of the Eleventh Central Committee [December 1978], the Party has returned to its correct policies in the economic, political, cultural and other fields. In addition, after a study of the new situation and new experience, it has adopted a series of correct new policies. Our Party now has a much deeper understanding of the laws governing China's socialist construction than it did at the time of the Eighth Congress, it has much more experience and is much more purposeful and determined to implement correct principles. We have every reason to believe that the correct programme that will be decided on at this Congress will create a new situation in all fields of socialist modernization and bring prosperity to our Party, our socialist cause, our country and the people of all our nationalities.

In carrying out our modernization programme we must proceed from Chinese realities. Both in revolution and in construction we should also learn from foreign countries and draw on their experience, but mechanical copying and application of foreign experience and models will get us nowhere. We have had many lessons in this respect. We must integrate the universal truth of Marxism with the concrete realities of China, blaze a path of our own and build a socialism with Chinese characteristics—that is the basic conclusion we have reached after reviewing our long historical experience.

China's affairs should be run according to China's specific conditions and by the Chinese people themselves. Independence and self-reliance have always been and will always be our basic stand. While we Chinese people value our friendship and co-operation with other countries and other peoples, we value even more our hard-won independence and sovereign rights. No foreign country should expect China to be its vassal or to accept anything harmful to China's own interests. We shall unswervingly follow a policy of opening to the outside world and actively increase exchanges with foreign countries on the basis of equality and mutual benefit. At the same time, we shall keep clear heads, firmly resist corruption by decadent ideas from abroad and never permit the bourgeois way of life to spread in our country. We, the Chinese people, have our national self-respect and pride. We deem it the highest honour to love our socialist motherland and contribute our all to her socialist construction. We deem it the deepest disgrace to impair her interests, dignity or honour.

The 1980s will be an important decade in the history of our Party and state. To accelerate socialist modernization, to strive for China's reunification and particularly for the return of Taiwan to the motherland and to oppose hegemonism and work to safeguard world peace—these are the three major tasks of our people in the 1980s. Economic construction is at the core of these tasks; it is the basis for the solution of our external and internal problems. For a long time to come, at least for the 18 years till the end of the century, we must devote every effort to the following four tasks: to restructure the administration and the economy and make our cadre ranks more revolutionary, younger, better educated and more competent professionally; to build a socialist civilization that is culturally and ideologically advanced; to combat economic and other crimes that undermine socialism; and to rectify the Party's style of work and consolidate its organization on the basis of a conscientious study of the new Party Constitution. These will be the most important guarantees that we shall keep to the socialist road and concentrate our efforts on modernization.

With 39 million members, ours is now a large Party playing a leading role in the exercise of state power. However, Communist Party members will always be a minority in the population as a whole. None of the major tasks proposed by the Party can be accomplished without the hard work of the people. Here, on behalf of the Party, I wish to pay high tribute to all the workers, peasants and intellectuals who have worked diligently for socialist modernization and to the People's Liberation Army—that Great Wall of steel safeguarding the security and socialist construction of our motherland.

China's democratic parties fought beside our Party in the period of the democratic revolution, and together with us they have advanced and been tested in the socialist period. In the construction work ahead our Party will continue its long-term co-operation with all patriotic democratic parties and individuals. On our Party's behalf, I wish to express sincere gratitude to all the democratic parties and to all our friends without party affiliation.

The cause of our Party has enjoyed the support and assistance of progressive people and friendly countries throughout the world. On behalf of our Party, I wish to express our sincere thanks to them also.

We must do our work carefully and well. We must strengthen our Party's unity with the people of all nationalities in our country and with the people of the world. We must struggle hard to make China a modern socialist country that is highly democratic and culturally advanced. We must also strive to oppose hegemonism, safeguard world peace and promote human progress.

DECIDE ON MAJOR CONSTRUCTION PROJECTS, MAKE PROPER USE OF THE TALENTS OF SCIENTISTS AND TECHNICIANS*

October 14, 1982

The goal to be achieved by the end of the century has been set: to quadruple the gross annual industrial and agricultural product in twenty years, on the basis of a steady improvement in economic efficiency.[1] Can it be achieved? The Twelfth National Congress of the Party says it can. And I also believe it can. But whether it really can be achieved depends on the success of our work in the years to come. At least, adequate preparations must be made over the next three years. In addition to construction projects envisaged in the plan, you have proposed a number of essential prospecting and design projects that are necessary to prepare for the construction projects themselves. Careful preparations must be made. Obviously, this means that energy and other key projects will have to be carried out. We must concentrate on these projects, whatever the difficulties. If money and materials are lacking, we must cut back local projects, especially those for ordinary processing industries. For no matter how many of these minor projects we complete, they won't amount to much.

These essential prospecting and design projects involve

---

* A talk with a senior comrade of the State Planning Commission.

many different trades and professions, and the relevant departments must attend to them and begin as soon as possible such preliminary work as scientific and technological research, technical and economic assessments, surveying and design. There must be a timetable for surveying and design, and there must be people in charge of making full preparations and monitoring the undertaking. Otherwise we won't be able to start, even when the money is available. This preliminary work has to be done before we can use foreign investment and invite foreign experts.

The period of twenty years is divided into two decades. The first decade prepares for the second. Preparation takes time, and we are in a race against time. We must be very serious about this. We must determine priorities among the various projects. We should concentrate our funds on projects that can be undertaken first. If some can be started a year earlier, we shall get benefits a year earlier. Things must not be allowed to drag on into the next century. Of course, some very large projects cannot be undertaken all at once.

Preliminary work includes the development of agriculture. Agricultural growth hinges first on policy and second on science. There are no limits to the development of science and technology or to the effect they can have. Seed, fertilizer and diversification all have great potential for development. Other things being equal, improved seed varieties will lead to a marked increase in production. Scientific use of fertilizers is also highly effective. And there are good prospects for fresh-water fishery. Some provinces abound in ponds and lakes. Farmers can get rich quickly by raising fresh-water fish to meet urban needs. The feed industry too must be developed. In addition to the application and development of relevant science and technology, plenty of organizational work is needed to improve seeds and promote the feed industry.

The preliminary work for the numerous major construction projects requires the mobilization of large numbers of scientists and technicians. Organizing these people to tackle key problems in science and technology is also a demanding task. We do have talented people, but the problem is how to organize them properly, arouse their enthusiasm and give scope to their talents. On the one hand, there is a great demand for scientists and technicians. On the other hand, highly trained people are often wasted because of poor organization. They are not assigned enough work, or cannot apply what they have learned or put their specialized skills to best use. We should consider the problem of organizing and managing scientists and technicians, because the present method of management doesn't work. It is quite a problem to find ways to use their talents and use them properly. Economically developed countries all attach great importance to this matter. Scientists and technicians are employed in national defence and civilian departments, scientific research units and institutions of higher education. There must be unified management if we are to break down the barriers between departments and between regions and make use of available talent. This cannot be done unless we have an authoritative organization in charge of scientists and technicians in both civilian and defence departments. Comrade Nie Rongzhen took such charge in the past, and things were in good order. Personnel could be transferred according to need and employed in large numbers for key projects. The first priority for quadrupling industrial and agricultural production in twenty years and implementing the policy towards the intellectuals is better management of scientists and technicians. This is the most pressing problem, and efforts should be made to solve it—and as quickly as possible.

Naturally, there is also the question of policy. People must be put in charge of planning, designing and approving all major construction projects. Each project must be undertaken by a small team of truly competent persons who will serve as a leadership core and be responsible for recruiting the rest of the staff. They will know where to find these people and how to organize them. If everything is left to the planning commission, the pace will be too slow. Some projects may be entrusted to universities or colleges, a number of scientists and technicians being transferred there to join in the work as needed. Competent people will come to the fore in the course of practice. They should be promoted unhesitatingly and placed in key posts. They will mature only if we are prepared to give them responsibility. With increasing numbers of skilled people, the outlook for our cause will be promising indeed. People of real ability should be especially promoted and given raises. On the other hand, those who year after year fail to produce anything useful can be transferred to other work with a cut in wages. We should increase material benefits for those who are talented or competent (not all intellectuals are). For their part, they should work conscientiously and to the best of their ability without fussing over their wages. But as far as the leadership is concerned, it should make an overall assessment of staff members and raise the wages of those who are deserving.

It is a good idea to invite people to apply for jobs. We have to devise standards and methods for selecting and appraising scientists and technicians.

OUR WORK IN ALL FIELDS SHOULD CONTRIBUTE TO THE BUILDING OF SOCIALISM WITH CHINESE CHARACTERISTICS*

January 12, 1983

According to latest statistics, gross industrial and agricultural production increased by 8 per cent in 1982, 4 per cent more than was planned. This raises a number of questions. What will come of achieving a much higher growth rate than projected in the annual plan? What has caused such a high growth rate? What are the major commodities that have been produced in excess of the plan? Will these products be overstocked? Will the high growth rate affect state investment in key development projects? We must investigate these questions right away and make an accurate analysis. However, this doesn't mean we should alter our Sixth Five-Year Plan. Long-term plans should be more flexible, while annual plans should be more specific, though of course they should have some flexibility too. Experience shows that whenever our plan was overambitious, we overreached ourselves. This has been a bitter lesson for us. We are already aware of this mistake and will continue to guard against it in future. But now we face the opposite situation. What happens when an excessive growth rate is achieved—excessive because the tar-

* Main points of a talk with senior comrades of the State Planning Commission, State Economic Commission, and the department in charge of agriculture.

gets were set too low? Nineteen eighty-two was the first year this happened. We must analyse this situation to find out why. We should pay close attention to the formulation of annual plans and not neglect it. And we should stress economic efficiency, instead of going after gross national product and percentage increases alone. In short, the principles for drawing up plans are: they should be specific, flexible and achievable if we work hard.

There should be a comprehensive plan for agricultural production. To quadruple agricultural output we should give priority to increasing grain production. But we cannot reach our goal if we concentrate solely on that. We must carefully work out the minimum amount of grain that will have to be produced in the year 2000 in order for each person to have enough. One way or another, we must reach this target in 2000. It is a goal of strategic importance. In China, each person usually consumes 200 to 250 kilogrammes of grain a year. The remainder goes for seed, animal feed and industrial uses. To produce adequate grain is no easy thing; it calls for efforts by several different sectors. The overall plan should include specific means by which to achieve this goal. For instance, there should be separate figures for the amount of additional grain to be produced through the use of more fertilizer, through the use of improved varieties of seeds, through better management, through improved capital construction and so on. Increased application of fertilizer is a reliable means of boosting production. The fertilizer should be of guaranteed quality. We should make it our policy to expand the chemical fertilizer industry. If we decide on this course, we must invest in chemical fertilizer plants. The selection of good seeds is another reliable method of increasing production. Take rice for example. Good hybrid seed varieties can increase rice production. Specialized seed companies should be established. They must have plots of land for experimentation and engage in scientific research. It should be required by law that good varieties of seeds be sown and that improved strains be regularly selected. The state should provide loans to poor rural areas in the form of seed and fertilizer. Capital construction in agriculture should be included in the plan. A timetable should be drawn up for all these endeavours and funds set aside for them. We must never forget that agriculture is the foundation of our economy.

To quadruple agricultural production we must depend primarily on diversification. There are two obvious directions to take: one is to develop animal husbandry and the other is to develop forestry and the growing of fruit. We should expand the raising of cattle, sheep, chickens and fish in the suburbs of large and medium cities. The state can provide support in the form of good breeding stock and feed. The whole nation should attend to feed processing. Several hundred modern feed plants should be built. Feed production should be treated as a sector of industry, and a major one.

Agriculture has great potential waiting to be tapped, but we haven't even started outlining general goals yet. Agronomists have made many good suggestions. We must step up scientific research and the training of competent personnel. We must apply science in all our endeavours to enhance crop yield per unit of area, to diversify agriculture, change methods of cultivation, solve the energy problem in rural areas, protect the environment and so on. We must focus our efforts on key projects in agricultural science.

Some people in rural areas and cities should be allowed to get rich before others. It is only fair that people should become prosperous through their own hard work. It is good for some people and some regions to become prosperous first, that development is supported by everyone. This new way is better than the old. In agriculture I favour the system of contracted responsibility for larger tracts of land. There is still something to be desired in this respect. The criterion for judging our work in all fields should be whether it contributes to the building of socialism with Chinese characteristics, to national prosperity and to the welfare and happiness of the people.

TAP INTELLECTUAL RESOURCES*

March 2, 1983

I recently travelled from Jiangsu to Zhejiang and from there to Shanghai. On this trip I found things were going very well. People were in high spirits. There were many new houses, there were plenty of consumer goods on the market, and cadres were brimming over with confidence. Prospects are obviously bright for our four modernizations. There should be more detailed planning for quadrupling the annual gross national product by the end of the century. Every province or municipality should have a specific plan so that it knows exactly what to do. We must help the provinces and municipalities solve their most pressing problems and thus create the conditions for completing their plans.

Industrial and agricultural output in Jiangsu Province has a gross annual value of over 73 billion yuan, that is, 1,200 yuan per capita or nearly double the per capita income of 1976. I asked comrades in Jiangsu how they had managed it. They said they had done two things. One was to rely on technicians from Shanghai. Many of them had retired and left Shanghai and were recruited in Jiangsu. They are highly skilled, and you don't have to pay much to get them. They are ready to accept work that brings them a little extra income and a few rooms to live in, and they have played an important role in increasing production. Many cities in Jiang-

*Excerpt from a talk with senior comrades of the Central Committee of the Chinese Communist Party.

su are no longer technologically inferior to Shanghai. Over the years comrades in Jiangsu have valued knowledge and intellectuals and so have put intellectuals' talents to good use. The other thing they did was to promote collective ownership, or in other words, to set up small and medium-sized enterprises.

Comrade Zhao Ziyang has suggested setting up economic co-operation zones, and everybody is happy about it. This is the right thing to do. In my view, economic zones should not be confined to Shanghai and Shanxi Province. Nor should we remain locked in an experimental stage. Progress would be too slow if we always made pilot studies on specific problems, taking several years to settle just a few problems. During the War of Liberation (1946-49) Comrade Mao Zedong held that the Second Field Army and the Third Field Army should be combined in military operations. He said that combining the two field armies would multiply their strength not just by two but several times over. The same is true of economic co-operation. It is true that many differences on the question of economic co-operation have yet to be resolved, but now is the time to start.

It is very important to tap intellectual resources. I include in this training for workers and managers, which should receive more attention. Universities and colleges should be expanded. In the near future, they should be expanded by 50, if not 100, per cent. This is well within our capacity. Doubling enrolments in key universities and colleges is not much of a problem. Teachers are not lacking. The main problem is housing. I think we can afford to spend a little more on college buildings and dormitories. We should calculate how much it would cost.

While there is an overall shortage of intellectuals, in some places young and middle-aged intellectuals find it difficult to play a useful role. We must resolve to implement the policy towards intellectuals, which includes improving their living standards.

BUILD A SOCIALIST SOCIETY WITH BOTH HIGH MATERIAL AND HIGH CULTURAL AND IDEOLOGICAL STANDARDS*

April 29, 1983

In a socialist country, a genuinely Marxist ruling party must devote itself to developing the productive forces and, with this as the foundation, gradually raise the people's living standards. This means building a society with high material standards. For a long time in the past we ignored the development of the productive forces, so now we are paying special attention to building a society with high material standards. At the same time, we are building a socialist society with high cultural and ideological standards, which essentially means that our people should be imbued with communist ideals, have moral integrity and a good general education and observe discipline. Internationalism and patriotism both belong to this realm.

---

* Excerpt from an interview with a delegation from the Central Committee of the Communist Party of India (Marxist).

THE PATH IS CORRECT AND THE POLICIES WON'T CHANGE*

June 18, 1983

The modernization we are striving for is modernization of a Chinese type. The socialism we are building is a socialism with Chinese characteristics. This is because we are acting according to our own concrete realities and conditions and mainly relying on ourselves.

Now that we are on the right track, our people are happy and we are confident. Our policies won't change. If they do, it will be only for the better. And our policy of opening to the outside world will only expand. The path won't become narrower and narrower but wider and wider. We suffered too much from taking a narrow road. If we turned back, where would we be headed? We would only be returning to backwardness and poverty.

The policy of abandoning the practice of "everybody eating from the same big pot" won't change. Industry has its distinctive characteristics, and so does agriculture; the experience of one can't be applied to the other. But the "responsibility system of determining remuneration according to output" remains our basic policy, of that you can be sure.

---

*Excerpt from a talk with foreign experts who attended the Symposium on Science and Technology Policies in Beijing in 1983.

AN IDEA FOR THE PEACEFUL REUNIFICATION OF THE CHINESE MAINLAND AND TAIWAN*

June 26, 1983

The most important issue is the reunification of the motherland. Peaceful reunification has become the common aim of the Kuomintang and the Communist Party. The idea is not that we swallow you up, or the other way round. We hope the two Parties will work together for national reunification and both contribute to the Chinese nation.

We do not approve of "complete autonomy" for Taiwan. There must be limits to autonomy, and where there are limits, nothing can be "complete". "Complete autonomy" means "two Chinas", not one. Different systems may be practised, but it must be the People's Republic of China alone that represents China internationally. We recognize that the local government of Taiwan has its own separate set of policies for domestic affairs. And although as a special administrative region Taiwan has a local government, it differs from local governments of other provinces, municipalities and autonomous regions. It enjoys certain powers of its own which other provinces, municipalities and autonomous regions do not possess, provided the national interests are not impaired.

After reunification with the motherland, the Taiwan special administrative region will assume a unique character and

*Main points of a talk with Professor Yang Liyu of Seton Hall University, South Orange, New Jersey, U.S.A.

may practise a social system different from that of the mainland. It will enjoy independent judicial power and there will be no need to go to Beijing for final adjudication. What is more, it may maintain its own army, provided it does not threaten the mainland. The mainland will not station anyone in Taiwan. Neither troops nor administrative personnel will go there. The Party, governmental and military systems of Taiwan will be governed by the Taiwan authorities themselves. A number of posts in the Central Government will be made available to Taiwan.

Peaceful reunification does not mean that the mainland will swallow up Taiwan. Needless to say, it doesn't mean that Taiwan will swallow up the mainland either. It is unrealistic to call for "reunification of China under the Three People's Principles".

There must be a proper way to bring about reunification. That is why we propose holding talks between the two Parties on an equal footing to achieve a third round of Kuomintang-Communist co-operation, rather than talks between the central and local governments. Once the two sides have reached an agreement, it can be formally proclaimed. But under no circumstances will we allow any foreign country to interfere. Foreign interference would simply mean China is still not independent, and that would lead to no end of trouble.

We hope the Taiwan authorities will consider carefully the nine principles proposed by Ye Jianying in September 1981[2] and Deng Yingchao's opening speech at the First Plenary Session of the Sixth People's Political Consultative Conference in June 1983[3] and that they will get over their misunderstanding.

In March of this year you held a forum in San Francisco on the prospects for China's reunification. That was a very good thing to do.

We shall complete the unfinished task left to us by our predecessors. If the Taiwan authorities can help to complete it, Chiang Kai-shek and his son and all those dedicated to the cause of China's reunification will have a better place in history. Of course, it takes time to bring about peaceful reunification. But it would not be true to say that we are in no hurry. People like us who are advanced in years wish to see reunification as soon as possible. We should have more contacts to enhance mutual understanding. We are ready to send people to Taiwan at any time, just to look around without any formal talks. And they are welcome to send people over here. Personal safety would be guaranteed and the whole thing would be kept confidential. We say all this in good faith. We do not play petty games.

We have achieved genuine stability and unity. Our principle of peaceful reunification of the motherland was formulated after the Third Plenary Session of the Party's Eleventh Central Committee. Related policies have been gradually defined. We shall adhere to them.

There has been some improvement in Sino-U.S. relations recently. However, those in power in the United States have never given up their "two Chinas" or "one-and-a-half Chinas" policy. The United States brags about its political system. But politicians there say one thing during a presidential election, another after taking office, another at mid-term election, and still another with the approach of the next presidential election. Yet the United States says that our policies lack stability. Compared with its policies, ours are very stable indeed.

USE THE INTELLECTUAL RESOURCES OF OTHER COUNTRIES*

July 8, 1983

We should make use of the intellectual resources of other countries by inviting foreigners to participate in key development projects and other construction projects in various fields and to assist in education and technical innovation. We haven't recognized how important to do this and consequently we haven't done as much as we should have. We shouldn't be reluctant to spend money on recruiting foreigners. It doesn't matter whether they stay here for a long time or a short time, or just for a single project. Let's invite them to come and help solve some problems. In the matter of modernization we lack both experience and technical know-how, so we should invite them to help us. We should make the best of their skills after they come here. In the past we gave them too many banquets and were too hesitant about asking for their advice and help, when in fact they were quite willing to assist us in our work.

---

*Excerpt from a talk with senior comrades of the Central Committee of the Chinese Communist Party.

INSCRIPTION FOR JINGSHAN SCHOOL

October 1, 1983

Education should be geared to the needs of modernization, the world and the future.

THE PARTY'S URGENT TASKS ON THE ORGANIZATIONAL AND IDEOLOGICAL FRONTS*

October 12, 1983

The major question before the current Plenary Session of the Central Committee has been the rectification of Party organizations. The Central Committee's decision on this question has been adopted after deliberation by all present. That decision is a very good one, and I fully agree with it. After the Session we shall discuss the Party's leadership on the ideological front. Now I should like to make two points: the rectification movement must not be conducted in a perfunctory way, and people working in the ideological field must not spread spiritual pollution.

Now, the first point: the rectification movement must not be conducted in a perfunctory way.

Since the Third Plenary Session of the Eleventh Central Committee, held in December 1978, our Party has reestablished Marxist ideological, political and organizational lines and formulated correct policies that are suited to actual conditions. Thus, excellent results have been achieved, new prospects are being opened up in every field of work and the masses have supported our Party's line and leadership. In the course of realizing this historic change, the Party members have repeatedly withstood the test of major struggles, and

---

* Speech at the Second Plenary Session of the Twelfth Central Committee of the Chinese Communist Party.

most of them have proved to be good, capable people, resourceful and ready to fight.

However, we are far from satisfied with the present state of affairs in the Party. There are still quite a few serious problems that we haven't had time to analyse and solve. Some negative things have been left over from the ten years of domestic chaos, and others have appeared and grown under the new historic conditions. The decision on rectification lists the "three types of people".[4] It also mentions people who have committed serious economic or other crimes, people who have abused power for private gain, people who have seriously impaired the Party's relations with the masses, people who have been at odds with the Party politically all along or who have merely pretended to be in agreement with it, and so forth. All these people are dangerous, corrupt elements, representing gross impurity in the Party's ideology, style of work and organization.

The most dangerous are the first three types. Some of them have been identified and dealt with, and others have corrected their ideology and conduct. But a certain number have simply lain low in the Party without ever renouncing their former stand. They are exceedingly dangerous for several reasons. First, they cling to their old factional mentality and are politically subversive, agitating against the Party. Second, they are cunning and deceitful; when the times are against them, they conceal their ideas to win other people's confidence, then when the situation changes in their favour, they will come forth to stir up trouble and fan the flames of unrest. Third, they have moved to different parts of the country and hidden out there, still maintaining their clandestine factional ties. And fourth, they are relatively young and well educated. After their downfall some of these people threatened to settle accounts ten or twenty years later. In short, they are a political force with unscrupulous ambition, and we must on no account take them lightly. They are walking time-bombs, and unless they are detected and defused during the rectification movement, they will destroy us.

It goes without saying that the other types of people listed are also dangerous and will be the ruin of us unless we deal with them now.

Many of our veteran Party members are deeply worried about this situation, and other people both inside and outside the Party are likewise concerned and indignant about it. Our entire membership and the people of all our nationalities are in favour of the decision made by the Twelfth National Party Congress to conduct Party-wide rectification, and they expect a great deal from the movement. Our Party must therefore be determined to carry it out thoroughly and conscientiously. We must see to it that we solve these serious problems and don't just go through the motions. We cannot let our Party comrades and the entire people down.

It was absolutely right for us to do everything possible to correct "Left" mistakes made during the "cultural revolution" and during previous political campaigns and ideological struggles. We shall never allow such mistakes to be repeated. However, quite a few comrades have made only a one-sided analysis of the historical lessons. They regard any mention of ideological struggle or of stern measures to be taken against people as a "Left" mistake and are only interested in combating "Left" mistakes and not Right ones. This leads to the other extreme, weakness and laxity. In waging ideological struggle against negative tendencies, persons and acts and in meting out organizational sanctions, Party people have tended in recent years to be a little too tolerant, hesitant, tender-hearted and ready to gloss things over to avoid trouble. Consequently, Party discipline has been so lax that some bad people were shielded.

Not long ago, concentrated efforts were made throughout the country to crack down swiftly on serious crime and to deal with offenders severely in accordance with the law. The people have been gratified by this and have given their warm support. They had been worried that if criminals were dealt with leniently and released like tigers sent back to the mountains, they might come back to avenge themselves. The people complained that we ought to have taken action earlier and criticized us for having waited so long. We should pay close attention to this reaction. Two years ago I pointed out that many leaders at various levels were weak and lax, as was shown by their tender-heartedness in dealing with persons guilty of grave criminal offences. They should draw a lesson from this reaction on the people's part and resolutely overcome their weakness and laxity. During the rectification movement, firm disciplinary measures must be taken against the three types of people mentioned earlier and against those who have made serious mistakes and caused great damage. Some of them should be expelled from the Party, others should be removed from office or subjected to other sanctions, as the case may be, and those who have committed crimes should be dealt with according to law. People who have made less serious mistakes should be severely criticized and should themselves make genuine, not superficial, self-criticisms and pledge to correct their failings. This will be one of the most important demonstrations that rectification is not being conducted in a perfunctory way.

During the rectification movement only a few Party members will be subjected to organizational sanctions. For the majority it will be only a matter of strengthening their Party spirit through ideological education. The purposes of the movement are to help the members make significant moral, ideological and political progress, to raise their awareness of the need to serve the people rather than to seek private gain, and to greatly improve relations between the Party and the masses. After the movement there should be regular criticism and self-criticism within the Party. All Party members, no matter who they are or what posts they hold, should be prepared to criticize others and themselves. The rectification movement should serve to strengthen Party organizations and bring about a fundamental improvement in the Party's style of work. All Party members, cadres and organizations are required to examine themselves in light of the qualifications set forth in the Party Constitution and to work out plans, in accordance with their own specific conditions, for meeting them, thus guaranteeing the implementation of the relevant provisions. Leading cadres at various levels, and senior cadres in particular, should set an example by strictly abiding by the Constitution and the "Guiding Principles for Inner-Party Political Life". This will be another important demonstration that the rectification movement is not being conducted in a perfunctory way.

In short, we must do a good job in the current rectification movement, so that our Party will become a militant Marxist party, a powerful central force leading the people throughout the country in their efforts to build a socialist society that is advanced materially, ideologically and culturally. With the firm resolve of our members, we shall surely succeed.

Now I come to my second point: people working in the ideological field must not spread spiritual pollution.

The ideological field covers a broad area, but I shall chiefly discuss theoretical work and literature and art. The past few years have witnessed great successes in these two fields. Our theorists have contributed a great deal by studying, expounding and propagating the theory that practice is the sole criterion of truth, the scientific analysis of the Party's history, especially in the period since the founding of the People's Republic, the building of socialism with Chinese characteristics, the reform of the economic and political structures, the building of a socialist society advanced in ideology and culture, and education in communism and patriotism. Many comrades in other academic fields have also been working hard and have made useful contributions. Our literature and art have never been so flourishing, and marked progress has been made in artistic expression and in the depiction of reality in all its breadth and depth. Excellent novels, pieces of reportage, poems, plays, films, television, dramas, musical compositions, paintings, dances and works of folk art have been produced. In this field, achievements have been predominant. There is no doubt about that, and it must be affirmed.

However, there are quite a few problems and much confusion among our theorists, writers and artists; in particular, some of them have spread spiritual pollution. So today I wish to discuss this question at some length.

All our workers fighting on the ideological front should serve as "engineers of the soul". In the effort to build a socialist society that is ideologically and culturally advanced and to promote the socialist cause as a whole, and particularly during the present period of change, they are charged with the heavy responsibility of educating people. The aftermath of the ten years of domestic turmoil, the difficulties left over from the past and the complicated problems that have arisen under the new circumstances have had different effects on people's thinking and have resulted in some confusion and misunderstanding. As "engineers of the soul", our ideological workers should hold aloft the banner of Marxism and socialism. They should use their articles, literary works, lectures, speeches and performances to educate people, teaching them to assess the past correctly, to understand the present and to have unshakable faith in socialism and in leadership by the Party. They should inspire the people to work hard, set high goals for themselves, have lofty ideals and moral integrity, raise their educational level, cultivate their sense of discipline and strive courageously for the magnificent cause of socialist modernization. This is what most ideological workers have been doing, to one degree or another. But some, flying in the face of the requirements of the times and our people, are polluting people's minds with unwholesome ideas, works and performances. In essence, spiritual pollution means the spread of all kinds of corrupt and decadent ideas of the bourgeoisie and other exploiting classes and the spread of distrust of socialism, communism and leadership by the Communist Party. The year before last the Central Committee convened a forum on problems in the ideological field, at which certain tendencies towards bourgeois liberalization and towards weakness and laxity in leadership were criticized. Some results were achieved after that forum, but not all the problems were solved. In some places leadership remained weak and lax, not all tendencies towards bourgeois liberalization were overcome and some even grew worse.

A number of theorists are indifferent to the major theoretical questions raised by socialist modernization. They are reluctant to investigate and study actual problems because, they say, they want to keep a distance from reality so as to avoid making mistakes, or because they think work of that sort is of no academic value. It is true that in the study of current problems some comrades have deviated from the Marxist orientation. They have engaged in discussions of the value of the human being, humanism and alienation and have only been interested in criticizing socialism, not capitalism. Of course, humanism may and should be studied and discussed as a theoretical and ethical question. But there are a thousand and one definitions of humanism. What we should do is make a Marxist analysis of it, disseminate and practise socialist humanism (which we used to call "revolutionary humanitarianism" during the years of revolution) and criticize bourgeois humanism. The bourgeoisie often boast how humane they are and attack socialism as inhumane. I am amazed to find that some of our Party comrades are preaching humanism, the value of the human being and so forth in abstract terms. They don't understand that neither in capitalist society nor in socialist society can there be an abstract value of the human being or abstract humanism, because even in our society there are still bad people, dregs of both the old and new societies, enemies of socialism and spies sent by other countries and Taiwan. It is true that the standards of living and education of our people are not high, but discussion of the value of the human being or of humanism isn't going to raise them. Only active efforts to achieve material, ideological and cultural progress can do that. Discussion of human beings apart from these specific conditions and tasks is discussion not of real human beings but of abstractions; this is not a Marxist approach, and it will lead young people astray. As to alienation, after Marx discovered the law of surplus value, he used this term only to describe wage labour in capitalist society, meaning that such labour was alien to the workers themselves and performed against their will, so that the capitalists might profit at their expense. Yet in discussing alienation some of our comrades go beyond capitalism; some even ignore the remaining alienation of labour under capitalism and its consequences. Rather, they allege that alienation exists under socialism and can be found in the economic, political and ideological realms, that in the course of its development socialism constantly gives rise to a force of alienation, as a result of the activities of the main body of the society. Moreover, they try to explain our reform from the point of view of overcoming this alienation. Thus they cannot help people to correctly understand and solve the problems that have arisen in socialist society today, or to correctly understand and carry out the continual reform that is essential for our technological and social advance. On the contrary, their position will only lead people to criticize, doubt and negate socialism, to consider it as hopeless as capitalism and to renounce their confidence in the future of socialism and communism. So what's the point of building socialism? they say. Marxist theory will advance and so will socialist theory; they will both advance as social practice and science advance. These comrades, however, are not advancing in their thinking but going backwards, back to pre-Marxist times. This confusion about humanism and the theory of alienation is a very serious problem among people working in the ideological sphere. And there are quite a few other problems of the same order. For instance, some people preach abstract democracy, even advocating free expression of counter-revolutionary views. They set democracy in opposition to Party leadership, put forward anti-Marxist arguments on the questions of Party spirit and service to the people, and so on. Even today there are still comrades who have doubts about the need to uphold the Four Cardinal Principles. For a while not long ago a few comrades doubted that our society was really socialist, that we should or could have a socialist system, and even that our Party was the party of the proletariat. Others argued that since we were still at the socialist stage it was only natural and correct for people to "put money above all else". Things came to such a pass that most of these mistaken ideas were published in newspapers and periodicals, and some have still not been clarified. All this goes to show the extent of ideological confusion that existed among theoretical workers.

So far as literature and art are concerned, it is gratifying that in recent years there have been more works depicting our new life as we strive to build socialism. There have been a number of pieces of reportage that awaken a revolutionary spirit, especially in young people, encouraging them to dedicate themselves to construction and struggle in every field, pieces that are very inspiring. There have been some inspiring works in other literary forms as well, but altogether there are not many. Some writers and artists have become indifferent to the socialist orientation and to the Central Committee's call for literature and art that serves the people and socialism. They are not interested in portraying and extolling the revolutionary history of the Party and the people and their heroic deeds in the struggle for socialist modernization. They do not proceed from the Party's revolutionary stand and try to help people understand the problems that have to be solved in the building of socialism, to inspire their enthusiasm and to strengthen their confidence. Instead, they make a point of writing about the dark side of life, they spread pessimism and sometimes even concoct stories to distort the revolutionary past and present. Others loudly praise the "modern" schools of thought of the West, declaring that the supreme goal of literature and art is "self-expression", propagating the notions of abstract human nature and humanism and maintaining that man's alienation under socialist conditions should be the theme of creative works. A few produce pornography. Although there are not many of these negative works, their influence on some young people cannot be ignored. Many writers and artists have neglected to study Marxism and held aloof from the people's struggle to build a new life, and some Party members have been reluctant to take part in Party activities. It is chiefly for these reasons that the negative phenomena have emerged.

The bad practice of putting money above all else has been spreading in literary and art circles. Some members of theatre troupes from the grass roots to the central level run around giving cheap performances and even staging low and vulgar shows just to make money. Most regrettably, certain famous actors and actresses, including some from the PLA troupes, have been swept up in this trend. It stands to reason that people are indignant about those persons who are interested only in catering to the bad taste of some audiences and who thereby sacrifice the honourable title of socialist writers and artists. And this tendency to regard money as the only important thing, to commercialize intellectual products, is manifested in other creative fields as well. Some who occupy positions in the fields of art and publishing or in departments in charge of cultural and historical relics have simply degenerated into merchants intent on nothing but profit.

What attitude should we take towards the bourgeois culture of the modern West? It is right for us to carry out the economic policy of opening to the outside world, and we must adhere to it for a long time to come. We must also continue to expand our cultural exchanges with other countries. With regard to economic exchanges, however, we are following a dual policy: we keep our doors open, but we are selective, we don't introduce anything without a purpose and a plan and we firmly combat all corrupting bourgeois influences. Why is it, then, that when it comes to cultural exchanges, we have allowed harmful elements of bourgeois culture to be introduced without impediment? It would be foolish to keep our doors closed and persist in the same old ways, if we want to learn from developed capitalist countries and take advantage of such advances in science, technology, management and other areas as may be useful to us. But in learning things in the cultural realm, we must adopt a Marxist approach, analysing them, distinguishing the good from the bad and making a critical judgement about their ideological content and artistic form. There are quite a few honest, progressive scholars, writers and artists in the West today who are producing serious and valuable works, which of course we should introduce into China. But some of our comrades rush to praise to the skies all trends in the philosophy, economics, socio-politics, literature and art of the West, without analysing them, distinguishing the good from the bad or exercising any critical judgement. There has been such confusion in the import of Western academic and cultural things that in recent years we have witnessed an influx of books, films, music, dances, and audio and video recordings that even in Western countries are regarded as pernicious junk. This corruption of our young people by the decadent bourgeois culture of the West is no longer tolerable.

It must be pointed out that the majority of our theorists, writers and artists are good or relatively good; only a few are guilty of spreading spiritual pollution. The problem is that the mistakes of those few have not been severely criticized and that necessary measures have not been taken to put a stop to their harmful actions and to the dissemination of their wrong ideas. Spiritual pollution can be so damaging as to bring disaster upon the country and the people. It blurs the distinction between right and wrong, leads to passivity, laxity and disunity, corrupts the mind and erodes the will. It encourages the spread of all kinds of individualism and causes people to doubt or even to reject socialism and the Party's leadership. The Four Cardinal Principles boil down to: upholding socialism and upholding the Party's leadership. These two principles are the basis for building our country and uniting all our people in a common struggle. Of course we should not attribute all negative phenomena—bad practices, criminal behaviour and the anti-socialist activities of a few—to ideological confusion, because there are many other reasons for them. However, we must not underestimate the impact of such confusion. Don't we all agree that practice is the sole criterion of truth? The comrades concerned should look at the influence and effects that their wrong words and actions, their pernicious writings and cheap performances have on young people and others. Our honest, sympathetic foreign friends are worried about these things. Of course there are also people—on the mainland, in Taiwan and Hongkong and abroad—who applaud them. I should like to give comrades concerned a bit of advice: when showered with praise, you should stop to think who it is that is applauding you, from what viewpoint and for what purpose, and put your work to the test of practice. Don't think that a little spiritual pollution doesn't matter much, that it's nothing to be alarmed at. Some of its ill effects may not be immediately apparent. But unless we take it seriously and adopt firm measures right now to prevent its spread, many people will fall prey to it and be led astray, with grave consequences. In the long run, this question will determine what kind of people will succeed us to carry on the cause and what the future of the Party and state will be.

The Party must strengthen its ideological leadership. The guiding principles laid down since the Third Plenary Session of the Eleventh Central Committee, and particularly at the Twelfth National Congress, are correct and clear-cut. The problem is that they have not been resolutely put into practice. Leading members of Party committees from the central to the local level must pay close attention to the situation among theorists, writers and artists, to the problems that have arisen in ideological work and to the way such work is done. First and foremost, they should recognize the seriousness of the problems and the urgent need to overcome weakness and laxity in leadership in this area. Some comrades are indifferent to spiritual pollution, they take a laissez-faire attitude towards it and even consider it something lively and colourful, an embodiment of the policy of letting a hundred flowers blossom, a hundred schools of thought contend. Others, knowing that it is wrong, are nevertheless reluctant to criticize it, because they are afraid of hurting people's feelings. This cannot go on. Just as we must take a serious and resolute attitude towards bad tendencies, persons and practices during the Party's rectification movement, so must we take the same attitude towards negative phenomena that give rise to ideological confusion and spiritual pollution. We must not stop half-way. The chief method for dealing with this confusion remains criticism and self-criticism. We must acknowledge that while our theorists, artists and writers have made a Marxist criticism of some negative tendencies, it has not yielded tangible results. For one thing, the criticism was insufficient in both quantity and quality, and for another, it met with substantial resistance. Inadequate as it was, it was often rejected as "an attack from all sides" or "coming down on people with a big stick", when in fact it was the critics who were attacked and the criticized who won sympathy and protection. This abnormal situation must change, so that propaganda in favour of socialism and communism will be truly predominant in the ideological sphere, along with the dissemination of Marxism and, in particular, of correct views on all major theoretical questions of principle. There are people who call their wrong views Marxist and others who challenge Marxism. Under these circumstances, Marxists should step forward and speak up. Party members working on the ideological front, particularly leading and influential ones, must stand in the forefront of the struggle. Those who have been mistaken themselves should make genuine self-criticisms and try to correct their thinking. Anyone who clings to his mistaken views and refuses to correct them cannot hold a leading position in ideological work. All Party members should strengthen their Party spirit and always abide by the Party Constitution and Party discipline. No matter whether they are scholars, writers, artists or specialists in any field, they are not allowed to consider themselves different from everyone else, wiser than the Party in political matters and free to do as they see fit. In the current rectification movement the most important task for Party organizations and members doing ideological work is to resolve these questions. Provided we make real efforts to reinforce Marxist leadership, to overcome weakness, laxity and the laissez-faire attitude and to wage active ideological struggle, all these problems can be readily solved.

When we try to do these things, people may wonder if the Party has changed its principles, if it has abandoned the policy of letting a hundred flowers blossom and a hundred schools of thought contend. The Party has not changed its principles, and it has not abandoned the "hundred flowers". To place criticism in contradiction to the "hundred flowers" policy is a gross misunderstanding or distortion. That policy is designed to enable socialist culture to flourish. Comrade Mao Zedong once said, "Truth develops through its struggle against falsehood. This is how Marxism develops." Some people took the "hundred flowers" policy to mean that there was absolute freedom to air any views, or even that only wrong views could be expressed, leaving no room for Marxist arguments. How can that be called letting a hundred schools of thought contend? They were turning the proletarian Marxist policy of the "hundred flowers" into a bourgeois policy of laissez-faire. Comrade Mao Zedong's *Oppose Liberalism* is a good Marxist essay. I suggest that leading comrades at all levels, especially those working in the field of ideology, study it conscientiously and act in accordance with it.

While stressing the need for active ideological struggle, we should continue to guard against "Left" mistakes. The ruthless methods used in the past—the over-simplified, one-sided, crude, excessive criticism and merciless attacks—must never be repeated. When speaking at meetings or writing articles, people should reason things out and analyse them rationally and scientifically. Those who are to take part in discussion or criticism should have clear ideas on the subject beforehand. They must on no account make sweeping criticisms, find something suspicious everywhere they look, use a position of power to intimidate others or try to convince them through sophistry. We should take a sympathetic attitude towards erring comrades, give them plenty of time for consideration and allow them to make reasonable reply, explaining the facts and clarifying their positions. We should particularly encourage sincere self-criticism and receive it warmly. It is good for a person to make such a self-criticism, and once he has done so, that should be the end of it. When criticizing either others or oneself, one should do it from a Marxist point of view, not from a "Left" point of view. We should continue to criticize and correct "Left" views in the ideological and theoretical sphere. But it should be clearly understood that the primary problem on the ideological front is to overcome the Right tendency to weakness and laxity.

In short, to strengthen Party leadership in ideological matters and overcome weakness and laxity has become an urgent task for the entire membership. Not only theorists, writers and artists but also people working in the fields of education, the press, publishing, radio and television and those doing cultural, ideological and political work among the masses are confronted with this task or other tasks that call for immediate action. All our ideological work has to be improved. We should put this question before the entire Party membership and give it an important place on the agenda of the Central Committee and of local Party committees at all levels. Now that we have shifted our emphasis to economic development, all our members should consider how to strengthen ideological work and adapt it to the new conditions, so that it is not neglected in favour of economic work. Party committees at all levels, and especially their leading members, must pay close attention to the situation on the ideological front, make a thorough study of the problems and adopt effective measures to improve work in this area. I suggest that the Political Bureau or the Secretariat of the Central Committee hold special discussions of that work, concentrating on principles, tasks, measures and so forth. I am convinced that if all our members recognize the importance of ideological work and give it their best efforts, and if at the same time we carry out the Party-wide rectification movement, a tremendous change will take place. A new situation will come into being in which socialist ideology and culture will flourish.

A NEW APPROACH TOWARDS STABILIZING THE WORLD SITUATION*

February 22, 1984

There are many disputes in the world, and we must find ways to solve them. Over the years I have considered how those disputes could be solved by peaceful means, rather than by war. The plan we have proposed for reunifying the mainland with Taiwan is fair and reasonable. After reunification, Taiwan can go on practising capitalism while the mainland maintains socialism, all within the same unified China. One China, two systems. The same approach will be applied to the Hongkong question—one China, two systems. But Hongkong is different from Taiwan in that it is a free port. I think this is a sensible solution to many disputes in the world. If opposing sides are locked in stalemate, sooner or later they will come to conflict, even armed conflict. If war is to be averted, the only alternative is the approach I have just mentioned, an approach the people will accept. It can help stabilize the situation, and for a long time too, and is harmful to neither side. Since you specialize in international issues, I hope you will have a better understanding of our proposal for the solution of the Hongkong and Taiwan questions and make a study of it. Anyhow, we must find a way out of this impasse.

I have also considered the possibility of resolving certain

---

* Excerpt from a talk with a delegation from the Center for Strategic and International Studies of Georgetown University in Washington, D.C.

territorial disputes by having the countries concerned jointly develop the disputed areas before discussing the question of sovereignty. New approaches should be sought to solve such problems according to realities.

I am just discussing offhand what has been on my mind. Is it possible to find new solutions for the many problems that cannot be solved by old ones? New problems should be solved by new means. Some of my remarks may not be precise or thoughtful enough. But we must rack our brains to find ways to stabilize the world situation. I have stated on many occasions that we Chinese are no less concerned about international peace and stability than people in other countries are. We need at least twenty years of peace to concentrate on our domestic development.

ON SPECIAL ECONOMIC ZONES AND OPENING MORE CITIES TO THE OUTSIDE WORLD*

February 24, 1984

I gathered some impressions from my recent tour of three special economic zones in Guangdong and Fujian provinces and of the Baoshan Iron and Steel Complex in Shanghai. Today, I have invited you here to discuss the policy of opening China to the outside world as it relates to the special economic zones and how to carry that policy a step further.

In establishing special economic zones and implementing an open policy, we must make it clear that our guideline is just that—to open and not to close.

I was impressed by the prosperity of the Shenzhen Special Economic Zone during my stay there. The pace of construction in Shenzhen is rapid. It is particularly fast in Shekou, because the authorities there are permitted to make their own

---

* Excerpt from a talk with several senior comrades of the Central Committee of the Chinese Communist Party after Comrade Deng Xiaoping returned to Beijing from an inspection tour of Guangdong and Fujian provinces and other areas. During his tour he wrote inscriptions in visitors' books for several of the places he visited. The one he wrote in Shenzhen was, "The development and experience of the Shenzhen Special Economic Zone prove the correctness of our policy of establishing such zones." In Zhuhai, he wrote, "The Zhuhai Special Economic Zone is a success." In Xiamen he wrote, "Manage the special economic zones in such a way as to achieve better and faster results." And for the Baoshan Iron and Steel Complex in Shanghai he wrote, "Master new technologies and techniques, be good at learning and better at innovating."

spending decisions up to a limit of U.S. $5 million. Their slogan is "time is money, efficiency is life". In Shenzhen, it doesn't take long to erect a tall building; the workers complete a storey in a couple of days. The construction workers there are from inland cities. Their high efficiency is due to the "contracted responsibility system", under which they are paid according to their performance, and to a fair system of rewards and penalties.

A special economic zone is a medium for introducing technology, management and knowledge. It is also a window for our foreign policy. Through the special economic zone we can import foreign technology, obtain knowledge and learn management, which is also a kind of knowledge. Probably not all the projects we've invested in will earn profits right away. But in the long run, we shall reap benefits. There are at least two things we can do now in Shenzhen: one is to build a nuclear power station, and the other is to establish a college with funds from overseas Chinese. They would be responsible for administering the college, inviting distinguished foreign professors to teach and purchasing teaching equipment from abroad. This would help us train a large number of competent people. If we manage this special economic zone successfully, offshore oil drilling will boom. The special economic zone will become the base for our open policy, and it will not only benefit our economy and train people but enhance our nation's influence in the world. Public order in Shenzhen is reportedly better than before, and people who slipped off to Hongkong have begun to return. One reason is that there are more job opportunities and people's incomes and living standards are rising, all of which proves that cultural and ideological progress is based on material progress.

The Xiamen Special Economic Zone is too small. It

should be expanded to cover all of Xiamen Island. If this is done, we shall be able to absorb investment from any foreigners and overseas Chinese. This will stimulate surrounding areas to service Xiamen, thus enhancing the economic development of all Fujian Province. The Xiamen Special Economic Zone will not be called a free port, although some free port policies could be implemented there. There are precedents for this. With the free flow of funds, foreign businessmen and overseas Chinese will invest there. I am sure this endeavour will not fail but will be very profitable.

In addition to existing special economic zones, we might consider opening more port cities, such as Dalian and Qingdao. We won't call them special economic zones, but policies similar to those in the zones could be pursued there. That would produce far more gains than losses. We should also develop Hainan Island. Successful economic development there would represent a substantial accomplishment.

Where shall we begin in developing China's economy? A Japanese friend has made two suggestions: First, that we begin with transport and communications, which are the starting points of economic development. Second, that we encourage high wages and high consumption. Being in a different situation from other countries, we are not in a position to adopt the second suggestion as our policy. However, as the special economic zones along the coast are developed successfully, we shall be able to increase people's incomes, which accordingly will lead to higher consumption. This is in conformity with the laws of development. It is a cardinal policy, and I hope all of us will give it some thought. Since conditions for the country as a whole are not ripe, we can have some areas become rich first. Egalitarianism will not work.

SAFEGUARD WORLD PEACE AND ENSURE DOMESTIC DEVELOPMENT*

May 29, 1984

The foreign policy which China has been pursuing in the 1980s and will continue to pursue in the 1990s and into the twenty-first century can be summed up in two sentences: First, we oppose hegemony in order to safeguard world peace. Second, China will always belong to the Third World, and this position is a foundation of our foreign policy. It means that China, being a poor country, belongs to the Third World as a matter of course, that it shares a common destiny with all Third World countries and that it will remain one of them even when it becomes prosperous and powerful, because China will never seek hegemony or bully others, but will always side with the Third World.

Among a host of problems in the present-day world, two especially stand out. One is the problem of peace. Now there are nuclear weapons; if war broke out, they could inflict untold losses on mankind. To work for peace one must oppose hegemony and power politics. The other is the North-South problem. It is very pressing at present. The developed countries are getting richer and richer while the developing countries are getting relatively poorer and poorer. If the North-South problem is not solved, it will hinder the recovery and development of the world economy. Its solution, of

---

* Excerpt from a talk with President Joao Baptista de Oliveira Figueiredo of Brazil.

course, lies in North-South dialogue. We support dialogue. But dialogue alone is not enough; co-operation among Third World countries—in other words, South-South co-operation—should be stepped up. Exchanges, learning from each other and co-operation among these countries can help solve many problems, and prospects are promising. The developed countries should appreciate that greater development of their economies is impossible without growth in the economies of Third World countries.

China's foreign policy is independent and truly nonaligned. China does not align itself with any country but invariably pursues a policy of independence. It will not play the "United States card" or the "Soviet Union card." Nor will it allow others to play the "China card". The aim of China's foreign policy is world peace. Always bearing that aim in mind, we are wholeheartedly devoting ourselves to the modernization programme to develop our country and to build socialism with Chinese characteristics.

China is still poor, with a per capita GNP of only U.S. $300. But we hope to increase this to $800 by the end of the century, which is a lofty goal. U.S.$800 is nothing to developed countries, but it really is an ambitious target for China, meaning a GNP of $1,000 billion at the end of the century. By then, China will be able to contribute more to mankind. As China is a socialist country, $1,000 billion will mean a higher standard of living for its people. More important, it will allow us to approach the standard of the developed countries in another 30 to 50 years' time. In short, we are now devoting ourselves wholeheartedly to the modernization of our country, and therefore we sincerely hope that no war will break out and that peace will be long-lasting.

ONE COUNTRY, TWO SYSTEMS*

June 22-23, 1984

The Chinese Government is firm in its position, principles and policies on Hongkong. We have stated on many occasions that after China resumes the exercise of its sovereignty over Hongkong in 1997, Hongkong's current social and economic systems will remain unchanged, its legal system will remain basically unchanged, its way of life and its status as a free port and an international trade and monetary centre will remain unchanged and it can continue to maintain and develop economic relations with other countries and regions. We have also stated repeatedly that apart from stationing troops there, Beijing will not assign officials to the government of the Hongkong special administrative region. This policy too will remain unchanged. We shall station troops there to safeguard our national security, not to interfere in Hongkong's internal affairs. Our policies with regard to Hongkong will remain unchanged for 50 years, and we mean this.

We are pursuing a policy of "one country, two systems". More specifically, this means that within the People's Republic of China, the mainland with its one billion people will maintain the socialist system, while Hongkong and Taiwan continue under the capitalist system. In recent years, China

---

* Summation of separate talks with members of a Hongkong industrial and commercial delegation and with Sze-yuen Chung and other prominent Hongkong figures.

has worked hard to overcome "Left" mistakes and has formulated its policies concerning all fields of endeavour in line with the principle of proceeding from reality and seeking truth from facts. After five and a half years things are beginning to pick up. It is against this background that we have proposed to solve the Hongkong and Taiwan problems by allowing two systems to coexist in one country.

We have discussed the policy of "one country, two systems" more than once. It has been adopted by the National People's Congress. Some people are worried that it might change. I say it won't. The crux of the matter is whether the policy is correct. If it is, it won't change; otherwise it will. Is there anyone who can alter China's current policy of opening to the outside world and invigorating its domestic economy? If it were changed, the living standard of 80 per cent of the Chinese population would decline, and we would lose these people's support. Therefore, the decisive factor is whether the policy is correct or not. If we are on the right track and enjoy the people's support, the policy will not change.

Our policy towards Hongkong will remain unchanged for a long time to come, but this will not affect socialism on the mainland. The main system in China must be socialism. The one billion people on the mainland will continue to live under the socialist system, but a capitalist system will be allowed to exist in certain areas, such as Hongkong and Taiwan. Opening a number of cities on the mainland and letting in some measure of capitalism will supplement the development of the socialist economy and benefit the growth of the socialist productive forces. For example, when foreign capital is invested in Shanghai, it does not mean that the entire city has gone capitalist. The same is true of Shenzhen [a special economic zone], where socialism still prevails. In China, socialism is the dominant system.

The concept of "one country, two systems" has been formulated to suit China's realities, and it has attracted international attention. China has not only the Hongkong problem to tackle but the Taiwan problem. What's the solution to the Taiwan problem? Is it for socialism to swallow up Taiwan, or for the "Three People's Principles"* preached by Taiwan to swallow up the mainland? The answer is neither. If the problem cannot be solved by peaceful means, then it must be solved by force. Neither side would benefit from that. Reunification of the motherland is the aspiration of the whole nation. If it cannot be accomplished in 100 years, it will be in 1,000 years. As I see it, the only solution lies in the implementation of two systems in one country. The world faces the choice between peaceful and non-peaceful means of solving problems. One way or the other, they must be solved. New problems must be solved by new means. The successful settlement of the Hongkong question may provide useful elements for the solution of international questions. Let's review world history. Is there any government that has ever pursued a policy as generous as China's? Is there anything recorded in the history of capitalism about any Western country doing something similar? When we adopt the policy of "one country, two systems" to solve the Hongkong question, we are not acting on impulse or playing tricks but are proceeding from reality and taking into full account the past and present circumstances of Hongkong.

We should have faith in the people of Hongkong, who are quite capable of administering their own affairs. The notion that Chinese cannot manage Hongkong affairs satisfactorily is a left-over from the old colonial mentality. For more than

* The Three People's Principles (nationalism, democracy and the people's livelihood) were put forward by Dr. Sun Yat-sen during China's bourgeois-democratic revolution.

a century since the Opium War, the Chinese people were looked down upon and insulted by foreigners. But China's image has been transformed since the founding of the People's Republic. The modern image of China was not created by the government of the Qing Dynasty, nor by the northern warlords,[5] nor by Chiang Kai-shek and his son. It is the People's Republic of China that has transformed China's image. All Chinese have at the very least a sense of pride in the Chinese nation, no matter what clothes they wear or what political stand they take. The Chinese in Hongkong share this sense of national pride. They have the ability to run the affairs of Hongkong well and they should be confident of this. The prosperity of Hongkong has been achieved mainly by Hongkong residents, most of whom are Chinese. Chinese are no less intelligent than foreigners and are by no means less talented. It is not true that only foreigners can be good administrators. We Chinese are just as capable. The view that the people of Hongkong lack self-confidence is not really shared by the people of Hongkong themselves. The contents of the Sino-British talks have not yet been made public, so many Hongkong residents do not know the Central Government's policy. Once they become familiar with it they will have full confidence. Our policy on the settlement of the Hongkong problem was made known by Premier Zhao Ziyang in his report on the work of the government to the Second Session of the Sixth National People's Congress, and it was approved by the congress. That shows how serious we are about it. If certain people remain stalled on the question of confidence or the credibility of the People's Republic of China and the Chinese Government, then nothing further can be accomplished. We are convinced that the people of Hongkong are capable of running the affairs of Hongkong well, and we want an end to foreign rule. The people of

Hongkong themselves will agree to nothing less.

Some requirements or qualifications should be established with regard to the administration of Hongkong affairs by the people of Hongkong. It must be required that patriots form the main body of administrators, that is, of the future government of Hongkong. Of course it should include other people, too, as well as foreigners invited to serve as advisers. Who are patriots? The qualifications for a patriot are respect for the Chinese nation, sincere support for the motherland's resumption of sovereignty over Hongkong and a desire not to impair Hongkong's prosperity and stability. Those who meet these requirements are patriots, whether they believe in capitalism or feudalism or even slavery. We don't demand that they be in favour of China's socialist system; we only ask them to love the motherland and Hongkong.

There is a span of 13 years between now and 1997. We should start working for a steady and smooth transition. First, major fluctuations or setbacks must be avoided and the prosperity and stability of Hongkong maintained. Second, conditions must be created for a smooth take-over of the government by Hongkong residents. I hope that people of all walks of life in Hongkong will work towards this end.

BUILD SOCIALISM WITH CHINESE CHARACTERISTICS*

June 30, 1984

Since the defeat of the Gang of Four and the convocation of the Third Plenary Session of the Party's Eleventh Central Committee, we have formulated the correct ideological, political and organizational lines as well as a series of principles and policies. What is the ideological line? To adhere to Marxism and to Marxist dialectical and historical materialism, or in other words, to seek truth from facts as advocated by Comrade Mao Zedong. Adherence to Marxism is vital to China and so is adherence to socialism. For more than a century since the Opium War,[6] China was subjected to aggression and humiliation. It is because the Chinese people embraced Marxism and kept to the road leading from New Democracy to socialism that the Chinese revolution was victorious.

People may ask: If China had taken the capitalist instead of the socialist road, could the Chinese people have liberated themselves and could China have finally stood up? The Kuomintang took that road for more than 20 years and proved that it does not work. By contrast, the Chinese Communists, by adhering to Marxism and integrating Marxism with actual conditions in China in accordance with Mao Zedong Thought, took their own road and succeeded in the

---

* Excerpt from a talk with the Japanese delegation to the second session of the council of Sino-Japanese non-governmental figures.

revolution by encircling the cities from the countryside. Conversely, if we had not been Marxists, or if we had not integrated Marxism with Chinese conditions and followed our own road, China would have remained fragmented, with neither independence nor unity. China simply had to adhere to Marxism. If we had not fully believed in Marxism, the Chinese revolution would never have succeeded. That belief was the motive force. After the founding of the People's Republic, if we had taken the capitalist rather than the socialist road, we would not have ended the chaos in the country or changed its conditions—inflation, unstable prices, poverty and backwardness. We started from a backward past. There was virtually no industry for us to inherit from old China, and we did not have enough grain for food. Some people ask why we chose socialism. We answer that we had to because capitalism would get China nowhere. We must solve the problems of feeding and employing the population and of reunifying China. That is why we have repeatedly declared that we shall adhere to Marxism and keep to the socialist road. But by Marxism we mean Marxism that is integrated with Chinese conditions, and by socialism we mean socialism that is tailored to Chinese conditions and has Chinese characteristics.

What is socialism and what is Marxism? We were not quite clear about this before. Marxism attaches utmost importance to developing the productive forces. We advocate communism. But what does that mean? It means the principle of from each according to his ability and to each according to his needs, which calls for highly developed productive forces and overwhelming material wealth. Therefore, the fundamental task for the socialist stage is to develop the productive forces. The superiority of the socialist system is demonstrated by faster and greater development of the productive forces than under the capitalist system. One of our shortcomings since the founding of the People's Republic was that we neglected the development of the productive forces. Socialism means eliminating poverty. Pauperism is not socialism, still less communism. The superiority of the socialist system lies above all in its ability to increasingly develop the productive forces and to improve the people's material and cultural life. The problem facing us now is how China, which is still backward, is to develop the productive forces and improve the people's living standards. This brings us back to the point of whether to continue on the socialist road or to stop and turn onto the capitalist road. The capitalist road can only enrich less than 10 per cent of the Chinese population; it can never enrich the 90 per cent. That is why we must adhere to socialism. The socialist principle of distribution to each according to his work will not create an excessive gap in wealth. Consequently, no polarization will occur as our productive forces become developed over the next 20 to 30 years.

The minimum target of our four modernizations is to achieve a comparatively comfortable standard of living by the end of the century. I first mentioned this with former prime minister Masayoshi Ohira of Japan during his visit here in December 1979. By a comfortable standard we mean that per capita GNP will reach U.S. $800. That is a low level for you, but it is really ambitious for us. China has a population of 1 billion now and it will reach 1.2 billion by then. If, when the GNP reaches $1,000 billion, we applied the capitalist principle of distribution, it wouldn't amount to much and couldn't help to eliminate poverty and backwardness. Less than 10 per cent of the population would enjoy a better life, while over 90 per cent remained in poverty. But the socialist principle of distribution can enable all the people to become relatively comfortable. This is why we want to uphold socialism. Without socialism, China can never achieve that goal.

However, only talking about this is not enough. The present world is an open one. China's past backwardness was due to its closed-door policy. After the founding of the People's Republic, we were blockaded by others, and so the country remained closed to some extent, which created difficulties for us. Some "Left" policies and the "cultural revolution" in particular were disastrous for us. In short, the experience of the past 30 years or more proves that a closed-door policy would hinder construction and inhibit development. Therefore, the ideological line formulated at the Third Plenary Session of the Party's Eleventh Central Committee is to adhere to the principles of integrating Marxism with Chinese conditions, seeking truth from facts, linking theory with practice and proceeding from reality. In other words, the line is to adhere to the essence of Comrade Mao Zedong's thought. Our political line focuses on the four modernizations, on continuing to develop the productive forces. Nothing short of a world war would make us release our grip on this essential point. Even should world war break out, we would engage in reconstruction after the war. A closed-door policy would not help construction. There are two kinds of exclusion: one is directed against other countries; the other is directed against China itself, with one region or department closing its doors to the others. We are suggesting that we should develop a little faster—just a little, because it would be unrealistic to go too fast. To do this, we have to invigorate the domestic economy and open up to the outside. We must first of all solve the problem of the countryside, which contains 80 per cent of the population. China's stability depends on the stability of the countryside with this 80 per cent—this is the reality of China from which we should proceed. No matter how successful our work in the cities is, it won't mean much without the stable base of the countryside. Therefore, we must first of all solve the problem of the countryside by invigorating the economy and adopting an open policy so as to bring the initiative of 80 per cent of the population into full play. We adopted this policy at the end of 1978, and after several years in operation it has produced the desired results.

The recent Second Session of the Sixth National People's Congress decided to shift the focus of reform from the countryside to the cities. The urban reform includes not only industry and commerce but science, education and all other professions as well. In short, we shall continue the reform at home. As for our relations with foreign countries, we shall pursue the policy of opening up still wider to the outside world. We have opened 14 medium and large coastal cities.[7] We welcome foreign investment and advanced techniques. Management is also a kind of technique. Will they undermine our socialism? Not likely, because the socialist economy is our mainstay. Our socialist economic base is so huge that it can absorb tens and hundreds of billions of dollars' worth of foreign funds without shaking the socialist foundation. Besides, we adhere to the socialist principle of distribution and do not tolerate economic polarization. Thus, foreign investment will doubtless serve as a major supplement to the building of socialism in our country. And as things stand now, this supplement is indispensable. Naturally, some problems will arise in the wake of foreign investment. But the negative aspects are far less significant than the positive use we can make of it to accelerate our development. It may entail a slight risk, but not much.

Well, those are our plans. We shall accumulate experience and try new solutions as new problems arise. In general, we believe the road we have chosen—building socialism with Chinese characteristics—is the right one and will work. We have followed this road for five and a half years and have achieved satisfactory results. We want to quadruple China's GNP by the end of the century. The pace of development has so far exceeded our projections. And so I can tell our friends that we are even more confident now.

THE "ONE COUNTRY, TWO SYSTEMS" CONCEPT WILL WORK*

July 31, 1984

The "one country, two systems" concept was not formulated today. It has been in the making for several years now, ever since the Third Plenary Session of our Party's Eleventh Central Committee held in December 1978. The idea was first presented as a means of settling the Taiwan and Hongkong questions. There are two ways available: non-peaceful and peaceful. The non-peaceful means, the use of armed force, is not desirable for either case. How, then, are these questions to be settled by peaceful means? Full consideration must be given to the history and present conditions of Hongkong and Taiwan. At the Third Plenary Session of the Eleventh Central Committee, Comrade Mao Zedong's principle of seeking truth from facts was reaffirmed, and that principle requires us to proceed from reality in everything we do. So, to respect facts or reality we have to respect the historical facts of Hongkong and Taiwan. When we propose that the capitalist system be preserved in Hongkong, we mean that the concept of "one country, two systems" can be applied there. The same is true of Taiwan. Our socialist system will not change, ever. But, if the capitalist system in Hongkong and Taiwan is not guaranteed, stability and prosperity there will be jeopardized, and peaceful settlement will be out of the question. There-

---

* Excerpt from a talk with the British Foreign Secretary, Sir Geoffrey Howe.

fore, first on the Hongkong question, we propose to guarantee that the current capitalist system and way of life will remain unchanged for 50 years after 1997.

The Chinese and British governments have reached a basic consensus in the talks on the Hongkong question. I am confident that the "one country, two systems" concept will work. International reaction to such a solution will be favourable, and the solution will set an example for other nations in settling the disputes history has bequeathed them. When we developed the concept of "one country, two systems", we also considered what methods should be used to resolve international differences. There are so many issues all over the globe that are tangled in knots and very difficult to solve. It is possible, I think, that some of them might be disentangled by this method. We have been trying to find mutually acceptable solutions to disputes. In the past, many flared up and led to armed conflicts. If fair and reasonable methods are applied, they will help eliminate flash points and stabilize the world situation.

SPEECH AT THE CEREMONY CELEBRATING THE 35TH ANNIVERSARY OF THE FOUNDING OF THE PEOPLE'S REPUBLIC OF CHINA

October 1, 1984

Comrade commanders and fighters of the Chinese People's Liberation Army! All fellow-countrymen, comrades and friends!

On this glorious occasion of the 35th anniversary of the founding of the great People's Republic of China, I wish to express my warmest congratulations to the comrades, compatriots and friends who are working for our socialist modernization, for the great cause of reunifying our motherland and for the security of our country.

Thirty-five years ago Chairman Mao Zedong, the great leader of the people of all our nationalities, solemnly proclaimed here the founding of the People's Republic of China. He declared that the Chinese people had finally stood up. In the past 35 years not only did we end a dark period of our history for all time and create a socialist society in China, but we have changed the course of human history. Particularly since the Third Plenary Session of the Eleventh Central Committee of the Chinese Communist Party, when the reactionary acts of the counter-revolutionary Gang of Four were definitely brought to an end, the approach of seeking truth from facts—a way of thinking advocated by Comrade Mao

Zedong—was restored and developed and a number of important policies suited to the new situation were adopted, the whole country has taken on a new look. On a foundation of national stability, unity, democracy and the rule of law, we have given socialist modernization the highest priority in our work. Our economy has grown more vigorously than ever before, and achievements in all other fields are widely acknowledged. Today, all our people are full of joy and pride.

The Party's Twelfth National Congress set a goal of quadrupling the gross annual industrial and agricultural product between 1980 and the year 2000. The experience of the past few years indicates that this magnificent goal can be reached. Our primary job at present is to reform systematically everything in the existing economic structure that is impeding our progress. At the same time, we shall carry out the planned technical transformation of existing enterprises throughout the country. We shall redouble our efforts in scientific and technological research, in education at all levels and in the training of workers, administrative staff and cadres. The entire Party membership and the community at large must truly value knowledge and let intellectuals make their contribution. All this will ensure that we shall gradually realize our modernization programme.

China's foreign policy is known to all, and it will remain unchanged. We stand firmly for the maintenance of world peace, for the relaxation of international tension and for arms reduction—above all, the reduction of the superpowers' nuclear and other weapons—and we are opposed to all forms of aggression and hegemony. China will remain open to the outside world and is ready to establish and expand diplomatic relations and economic and cultural ties with all countries on the basis of the Five Principles of Peaceful Coexistence. We believe in settling international disputes through negotiations, as China and the United Kingdom have done with regard to the Hongkong question. In the seriously deteriorating international situation, we must strengthen our national defence. All commanders and fighters of the Chinese People's Liberation Army must be alert at all times, constantly upgrade their political and military quality and strive to master the skills of modern warfare.

We want peaceful reunification with Taiwan, which is part of our sacred territory. Our policy in this regard is also known to all and will not change. The desire for peaceful reunification of the motherland is taking hold in the hearts of all descendants of the Yellow Emperor. It is an irresistible trend, and sooner or later it will become a reality. We hope that the people of all our nationalities, including our compatriots in Hongkong, Macao and Taiwan and those residing abroad, will work together for its early realization.

Long live the great People's Republic of China!

Long live the great Communist Party of China!

Long live the great Chinese People's Liberation Army!

Long live the great unity of all nationalities of China!

MAINTAIN PROSPERITY AND STABILITY IN HONGKONG*

October 3, 1984

With so many of you attending our National Day celebrations, I believe Hongkong has a bright future. Among those who have come for the celebrations are people from different professions and walks of life and with differing political views. This shows that you all favour China's resumption of the exercise of sovereignty over Hongkong and the agreement reached between the Chinese and British governments. It follows that we share the same objective, a common goal of maintaining prosperity and stability in Hongkong over the next 13 years and beyond, which means in essence that we share the same love of our motherland and love of Hongkong. I am extremely happy to have so many visitors. With our joint effort, I am sure our goal will be achieved. After 1997 those of you who are sixty or seventy will not be as energetic as you are today. There are many young people among us here. They have an advantage over us in this respect. As for me, I would love to be around in 1997, to see with my own eyes China's resumption of the exercise of sovereignty over Hongkong.

Some people are worried that China's policy may change once we are no longer around. I appreciate their trust in elderly men like me. But today I would like to assure you that

---

* Excerpt from a talk with Chinese from Hongkong and Macao attending the National Day celebrations in Beijing.

China's policy will not change; nobody can change it, because it is right and effective and enjoys the support of the people. Since it is backed by the people, anyone who tries to change it will meet with the people's opposition. Moreover, our Central Government and the Central Committee of the Communist Party always live up to their international obligations, and that was true even during the years of turbulence. Acting in good faith is a Chinese tradition, not something invented by our generation. It is an essential quality of our magnificent old country. Ours is a great and proud nation. And a great nation should preserve its dignity and adhere to the principles it has formulated. In the agreement we stated that no change would be made for 50 years, and we mean it. There will be no changes in my generation or in the next. And I doubt that 50 years after 1997, when the mainland is developed, people will handle matters like this in a narrow-minded way. So don't worry, there won't be any changes. Or if there are, they can only be changes for the better, for the greater benefit of the prosperity and growth of Hongkong, not changes detrimental to the interests of the people there.

With regard to the Sino-British joint declaration, we know that we shall abide by it, we are convinced that the British will do the same and we are still more convinced that the overwhelming majority of our Chinese compatriots in Hongkong will do so too.

After 1997 Taiwan's institutions in Hongkong may still remain there. They will be able to disseminate their "Three People's Principles" and criticize the Communist Party —which does not bother us, because the Communist Party cannot be toppled by criticism. However, I hope they will take care not to create disturbances in Hongkong or to advocate "two Chinas", which is no longer just a matter between the mainland and Taiwan, but a question of international significance. We believe that, being Chinese, they will stand on the side of our nation and help safeguard its general interests and dignity. They will be allowed to carry out their activities and conduct propaganda in conformity with the requirements mentioned above.

It is my hope that our compatriots from Hongkong and Macao will visit more places and see more of our country to witness the changes. We have a slogan, "Long live the great unity of the Chinese nation", right? All the people, regardless of their differing political views, including those who criticize the Communist Party, should unite. I hope that our compatriots in Hongkong will unite and pool their efforts to safeguard prosperity and stability in Hongkong, so as to contribute to a smooth transfer of political power in 1997.

"One country, two systems" is a new concept internationally. We proposed this policy not just because we are faced with the Hongkong question, but also because the general objective of our foreign policy is to safeguard world peace. New approaches are needed for resolving international disputes in the present-day world. Naturally, the success of "one country, two systems" depends on the efforts of our compatriots in Hongkong, and I am convinced that time will bear witness to that success.

THE MAGNIFICENT GOAL OF OUR FOUR MODERNIZATIONS, AND OUR BASIC POLICIES*

October 6, 1984

I am a layman in the field of economics. I have made a few remarks on the subject, but all from a political point of view. For example, I proposed China's economic policy of opening to the outside world, but as for the details or specifics of how to implement it, I know very little indeed. So today I am dealing with the question again from the political point of view.

We have determined a political objective: to quadruple economic production by the end of the century, with a per capita gross national product of U.S. $800 and a better standard of living for our people. I put forth this idea in an interview with a Japanese friend, Masayoshi Ohira, who was then prime minister of Japan. During his visit to Beijing in 1979, he asked me about the aim of our four modernizations. I answered that we would probably try to quadruple production by the end of the century. China's per capita GNP in 1979 was about $250, and in 2000 it would be $1,000, a fourfold increase. Later, I took into account the fact that our population would not remain at 1 billion but would be 1.2 billion by then, according to our rough estimates, which would mean a little more than $800 per capita. It follows that

* An interview with Chinese and foreign delegates to a symposium on China's economic co-operation with foreign countries.

the Chinese people will enjoy a more comfortable life. This goal may seem modest to developed countries, but to China it is a very ambitious, magnificent goal. Its achievement will mean a GNP of $1,000 billion. What is more important, such a huge sum will provide a solid foundation for our attempt to approach the level of the developed countries within 30 to 50 years. And this is no easy job, either. Bragging and empty talk will accomplish nothing. We need to have a whole set of sound guidelines and policies concerning domestic and foreign affairs. Since the Third Plenary Session of our Party's Eleventh Central Committee, we have formulated a policy of invigorating the domestic economy and opening to the outside world. Our goal cannot be attained without this policy.

We began with the countryside. Eighty per cent of our population lives there. China's social stability and its economic development depend above all on the development of the countryside and the improvement of rural living standards. A fourfold increase in production depends first and foremost on whether it can be achieved by the 80 per cent of our people who live in the countryside. It seems that all our rural policies are succeeding and rapidly bringing about excellent results. In the past, life in the countryside was rather difficult. Now we can say that most of our people there have enough food to eat and clothes to wear, and their housing conditions have greatly improved. The success of our rural policies has heightened our confidence and encouraged us to strive for our target of quadrupling the GNP.

The recent rural reforms are of revolutionary significance. Meanwhile, we have embarked on an experiment in urban reform. Of course, we cannot mechanically apply what is working in the countryside to the cities, where the situation is far more complex, involving industry, commerce and the service sector as well as the scientific, educational and cultural spheres. Urban reforms and the restructuring of the economy in general will be the main topic for the forthcoming Third Plenary Session of the Twelfth Central Committee of the Party. That session will herald China's comprehensive reform. It took three years for rural reform to take effect, and it may take three to five years for urban reform to bring about noticeable changes. Our experience in the countryside convinces us that our urban reform will succeed. We are aware that mistakes may be made because of the complicated nature of urban reform, but they will not affect the situation as a whole. We shall watch our step, and if anything goes wrong, we shall put it right, that's all. In short, we shall adhere to our motto, seek truth from facts. We are convinced that our urban reforms will succeed too and that the forthcoming Third Plenary Session of the Twelfth Central Committee will go down in Chinese history as a very important event.

While invigorating the domestic economy, we have also formulated a policy of opening to the outside world. Reviewing our history, we have concluded that one of the most important reasons for China's long years of stagnation and backwardness was its policy of closing the country to outside contact. Our experience shows that China cannot rebuild itself with its doors closed to the outside and that it cannot develop in isolation from the rest of the world. It goes without saying that a large country like China cannot depend on others for its development; it must depend mainly on itself, on its own efforts. Nevertheless, while holding to self-reliance, we should open our country to the outside world to obtain such aid as foreign investment capital and technology. This kind of assistance is not unilateral. While China will obtain investment capital and technology from other nations, particularly the developed ones, it will in turn make a greater contribution to the world economy. Its expanded foreign trade in recent years has borne this out. So we say that the assistance and the contribution are mutual.

Invigorating our domestic economy and opening to the outside world are our long-term, not short-term, policies that will remain unchanged for at least 50 or 70 years. Why? Because quadrupling the GNP, which will take 20 years, is only our first step and will be followed by a second, approaching the level of developed countries, which will take 30 or 50, let's say 50, years. The two steps together will take 50 or 70 years. By then chances for changes in the policy will be even slimmer. If anything, we shall open up still more. Our people would not allow anything else.

It is our hope that businessmen and economists in other countries will appreciate that to help China develop will benefit the world. China's foreign trade volume makes up a very small portion of the world's total. If we succeed in quadrupling the GNP, the volume of our foreign trade will increase considerably, promoting China's economic relations with other countries and expanding its market. Therefore, judged from the perspective of world politics and economics, China's development will benefit world peace and the world economy. Western statesmen should realize that unless it helps developing countries, the West will have difficulties solving its own problems of markets and economic development. An open economic policy is not a question confronting just the developing world, but developed nations, too, I am afraid. Three-fourths of the world's population live in the developing countries, an area which does not yet amount to much in terms of a market. But there is only limited room for expanding the world market if we confine ourselves to the developed countries alone.

We hope that foreign industrialists and businessmen will

consider co-operation with China in a world perspective. Co-operation has been proceeding quite well in recent years. We need to expand it. China will work to encourage it, and so should the industrialists and businessmen of developed nations. First of all, they should set aside their concern about risks; there is no need to worry that our policies might change. They should confidently accelerate the pace of co-operation with us. Time will prove that those who help us will benefit no less in return. And their help will have even greater significance politically and strategically.

To facilitate extensive contact, the China International Trust and Investment Corporation can serve as a window to the outside world.

Believe me, the Chinese people are not petty-minded about details. Some of our laws are not yet well defined because we lack experience, but they will be as time goes on. In the course of discussions, some friends have expressed their fear of risks. If any problems arise, we shall share the burden. Others have raised the question of the duration of co-operation between enterprises. If the technology and techniques you provide are really advanced, co-operation can be prolonged.

SPEECH AT THE THIRD PLENARY SESSION OF THE CENTRAL ADVISORY COMMISSION OF THE COMMUNIST PARTY OF CHINA*

October 22, 1984

I think the current Central Committee is an experienced one and has been able to handle different kinds of problems well. Foreign newspapers stress my role in it. True, I have a part in it, but most of the work is being done by other comrades. I have offered some advice, but it is comrades in charge of the day-to-day work who are performing the hardest tasks and dealing with individual problems in an orderly fashion. Take, for example, the "Decision on Reform of the Economic Structure" adopted by the Twelfth Central Committee of the Party at its Third Plenary Session. There has been a good deal of reaction to that document in the past two days. Everyone says it is of historic significance. It's a good document, but I didn't write or revise a single word of it. All this is true. Don't try to exaggerate my role. That would only raise doubts in people's minds and lead them to believe that our policy will change once Deng is gone. The world community is quite concerned about this. Others say that the policy will not change as long as Hu Yaobang[8] and Zhao Ziyang[9] are around. This sounds better. However, Yaobang is 69 years old and Ziyang is 65, both approaching 70. We

---

* Slightly abridged for publication.

should make it very clear to the rest of the world that nobody can alter the principles, policies and strategies we have worked out. Why? Because experience has demonstrated their soundness. If they were changed, the country and the people would suffer. So the people would never agree to change them. We say our current policy is working, because our country is thriving, the people's living standards are genuinely rising and China's international prestige is growing. These are the essential facts. Our policy succeeded first in the countryside. It will not change there. If it did, 800 million peasants would oppose it, because their living standards would immediately decline. There are still some tens of millions of peasants in the countryside who do not yet have enough food or clothing, although things are much better than before. The Central Committee has mapped out a plan to help the poor areas to prosper. Now that most parts of the country have become better off, the state can spare more resources to help develop the rest. This problem will not be too difficult to solve, because the prosperous areas too can lend a helping hand. We know from our own experience that our generation, including Yaobang and Ziyang, would not change this policy. Nor would the third, fourth or fifth echelons of cadres, because nobody could. In recent talks with foreign guests, I never failed to assure them that our policy would not change, that they could rely on the continuity of our current policy. Still, they were not thoroughly convinced. This is a serious problem of which I am well aware. And that's why I have adopted a lighter work schedule. Its advantages are: first, I will enjoy a longer life; and second, others are doing more work than I am and doing it well—better than I, in fact, because they are full of vigour. I hope I shall gradually give up work altogether and maintain my good health. Then I shall have fulfilled my mission. But for now I still have to do some work. Last year I devoted myself to only one thing: a crackdown on criminals. This year I worked on two projects: one was to open another 14 cities; the other was to resolve the Hongkong question through the "one country, two systems" approach. Everything else was done by other people.

The policy of "one country, two systems" has been adopted out of consideration for China's realities. China is faced with the problems of Hongkong and Taiwan. There are only two ways to solve them. One is through negotiation and the other is by force. To solve a problem by peaceful negotiation requires that the terms be acceptable to all parties. The solution to the Hongkong question, for instance, should be acceptable to China, Britain and the people of Hongkong. What will they accept? A socialist transformation of Hongkong would not be acceptable to all parties. In my talks with foreign guests I proposed that new solutions to international disputes be devised to meet new situations and new problems. The "one country, two systems" concept was proposed on the basis of Chinese realities, but this idea could also be applied to international problems. International disputes that are not handled right can reach the flash point. I asked them whether the policy of "one country, two systems" could be adopted in some cases and the policy of "joint development" in others. In this way we would not be confined to just one approach, the "one country, two systems". We would have an alternative in "joint development". We Chinese stand for peace and hope to solve disputes by peaceful means. What kind of peaceful means? "One country, two systems" and "joint development". Everyone says this is a new and very interesting idea.

The resolution of the Hongkong question was due not so much to any special feats on the part of our negotiators as to the fact that China has been progressing rapidly. In recent years it has been thriving and growing powerful and has proved trustworthy. We mean what we say and we keep our word. Since the fall of the Gang of Four, and especially since the Third Plenary Session of the Eleventh Central Committee, highly favourable changes have taken place in China. Its image has improved. The past five years have witnessed great changes. Our own people have seen this, and so have people from other countries. We can be proud of this. Of course, there is a difference between pride and conceit. We should not be conceited or boastful, because we are still economically backward. But recent developments, the resolution of the Hongkong question for instance, demonstrate our good prospects as a nation. That resolution was achieved because we adopted a fundamentally correct policy or strategy of "one country, two systems". It was also the result of the combined efforts of the Chinese and British governments.

The resolution of the Hongkong question has a direct bearing on the Taiwan question. The Taiwan authorities should be able to accept the "one country, two systems" concept. Is it realistic of Jiang Jingguo to propose unifying China under the "Three People's Principles"? His "Three People's Principles" were applied in China for 22 years —from 1927 to 1949. What became of China? When did the Chinese people stand up? In 1949. It was socialism and the Communist Party that made it possible for the Chinese people to stand up. Isn't "one country, two systems", an arrangement whereby you won't swallow us up and we won't swallow you up, a better solution? Recently, a foreigner asked me whether we would adopt a similar policy towards Taiwan. I said that in Taiwan's case we would adopt an even more flexible policy. By more flexible I meant that in addition to the policies used to settle the Hongkong question, we would allow Taiwan to maintain its own armed forces. A couple of days ago I discussed Taiwan with another foreign visitor. I said we would strive to solve the Taiwan question by peaceful means but we could not possibly rule out the use of non-peaceful means to reunify Taiwan and the mainland.

Let me turn to domestic economic development. As I said earlier, the members of the current Central Committee are working together smoothly. The situation as a whole is very good. Isn't it stated in the "Decision on Reform of the Economic Structure" that political unity and stability in China are increasing? This is quite true. How often since its founding has our Party experienced as good a political situation as this? In my talk with foreign visitors, I was bold enough to say that we would quadruple our industrial and agricultural output by the year 2000. We never dared to be so positive before. Instead, we said only that with strenuous efforts a fourfold increase might be possible. Four years later, we find that the major targets of the Sixth Five-Year Plan (1981-85) were reached two years ahead of time. This year's annual plan will be surpassed. We used to say that a fourfold increase would be realized if the average growth rate reached 6.5 per cent for the first 10 years and 7.2 per cent for the 20 as a whole. Now it seems that the average growth rate for the first 10 years may exceed 7.2 per cent, because the growth rate over the last three years reached nearly 8 per cent.

Quadrupling the gross national product is very important. This would mean an annual GNP of U.S. $1,000 billion by the year 2000. At that time China's GNP will rank it among the advanced countries in the world, though not, of course, on a per capita basis. In terms of people's living standards, $1,000 billion will mean a comfortable life, and in terms of national strength, China will be more powerful. If we allocate 1 per cent of this sum to national defence, that means $10 billion; 5 per cent means $50 billion. With $10 billion we could accomplish a lot of things, and it would be easy to upgrade our military equipment. If we devoted 1 per cent of this total to science and education, we could run many universities, and we would also have more funds to spend on the elimination of illiteracy. The investment in intellectual resources must exceed 1 per cent. Now we face too many difficulties and find it hard to add even a small amount to education and scientific research. Our people will be more prosperous by the end of the century, enjoying a much higher living standard than they do now. Last year I toured Suzhou. The industrial and agricultural output of the Suzhou area reached a per capita value of approximately $800. If calculated in terms of the gross national product, its per capita income would be $400. I investigated life in Suzhou. First, people there don't want to leave for Shanghai or Beijing. Probably people in most parts of Jiangsu Province are happy with their lives and would rather not leave their hometowns. Second, average living space exceeds 20 square metres per person. Third, everybody has received at least a primary education because the people have more money to spend on schools. Fourth, people have no more problems with food or clothing, they generally own television sets, other household appliances and what not. Fifth, there has been a dramatic change in people's attitude towards life, and disorderly conduct and the crime rate have declined significantly. There are other improvements that I can't recall now. But the ones I just listed are great enough! For now, we shall continue our efforts to crack down on criminals. By the year 2000, people's attitude towards life will be quite different. Material conditions are the foundation. With improved material conditions and a higher cultural level, people's attitude towards life will improve greatly. Our effort to bring criminals to justice is necessary and we shall continue it. But the ultimate solution lies not in such an effort, but in quadrupling the GNP. Of course, even then we shall still have to conduct education among the people; work among the people can never be dispensed with. But we shall have paved the way for all our other efforts. We can confidently say we shall quadruple the GNP. What will the political situation be like once we have achieved that? I think there will definitely be genuine stability and unity. Now the situation is becoming increasingly stable. By that time, China will be truly powerful, exerting a much greater influence in the world. We have to work hard for 20 years. There are 16 more years until the year 2000. Let's apply ourselves and work with one heart and one mind.

Quadrupling production is significant in another way. It will provide a new starting point from which, in another 30 to 50 years, we shall approach the level of the developed countries. This refers to production and living standards, not to political systems. It is something feasible, tangible and within our grasp. In my recent interviews with foreigners, several of them asked whether, when we said we would not change Hongkong for 50 years, we had any particular reason for choosing that figure. I answered that we had. We shall set a new target after quadrupling the GNP by the end of the century, namely, to approach the level of the economically developed countries within another 30 to 50 years. Why are we thinking in terms of 50 years beyond 1997? Why do we say that opening China to the outside world and absorbing foreign investment capital are long-term policies which, as far as Hongkong is concerned, will remain unchanged for at least 60 or 70 years from now? Because we want to quadruple our GNP and then reach a new target, and we cannot do either without an open policy. We can easily illustrate this point by considering just one aspect of the question. Our foreign trade volume is now at $40 billion, right? How can we quadruple production from such a meagre base if we pursue a closed-door policy? This aspect alone suffices to drive the point home. As simple as that. Of course we can cite many others too. For example, what shall we do with our products when our GNP reaches $1,000 billion? Are we going to sell them all on the domestic market? And are we going to produce at home everything that we need? Naturally, we are going to import what we need and export our products. If we don't open up to the outside world, it will be difficult to quadruple production and even more difficult to make progress after that. Foreigners worry that we may change our policy of opening to the outside world. I have said it will not change. I have told them that our first target covers the period between now and the end of the century and that we have a second target to achieve within 30 to 50 years or maybe longer, say 50 years, in which this policy will not be abandoned. Isolation prevents any country's development. We suffered from this and so did our forefathers. You might say it was an open policy of a sort when Zheng He was sent on voyages in the western oceans by the Ming Emperor Zhu Di (who reigned from 1402 to 1424).[10] But the Ming Dynasty entered a decline with the death of Emperor Zhu Di and China was subjected to foreign aggression. In the Qing Dynasty, during the reign of Kang Xi (1662-1722)[11] and that of Qian Long (1736-95) there was no open policy to speak of. Isolation lasted more than 300 years, from the middle of the Ming Dynasty (1368-1644) to the Opium War (1840). Counting from the reign of Kang Xi, it was almost 200 years. As a result, China fell into poverty and ignorance. After the founding of the People's Republic, we did open our country to the outside world during the First Five-Year Plan period, but only to the Soviet Union and East European countries.

Later we closed our doors and economic development slowed down. Of course there were other reasons: for instance, we made mistakes. We must open ourselves to the outside world. It will not hurt us. Some of our comrades are always worried that undesirable things may happen if we do that. Above all, they worry that the country might go capitalist. I'm afraid some of our veteran comrades do harbour such misgivings. Since they have devoted their lives to socialism and communism, the spectre of capitalism horrifies them. Hence their misgivings. But such a thing will not happen. Still, there will be some negative effects. We must be alive to them, although they are not difficult to overcome. If we practise isolationism and close our doors again, it will be absolutely impossible for us to approach the level of the developed countries in 50 years. When our per capita GNP reaches several thousand dollars, no new bourgeoisie will emerge, because such essential things as the means of production will still be state-owned or publicly owned. And if the country prospers and the people's material and cultural life continually improves, what's wrong with that? However much we open up in the next 16 years before the end of the century, the publicly owned economy will remain predominant. Even in a joint venture with foreigners, half is socialist-owned. And we will take more than half of the actual earnings from joint ventures. So, don't be afraid. It is the country and the people who will benefit most from them, not the capitalists. Negative effects are inevitable but we can deal with them. "Decision on Reform of the Economic Structure" is a very good document, for it explains what socialism is in terms never used by the founders of Marxism-Leninism. There are some new theories. I think the document has clarified things. We could not have drawn up such a document before; without the experience of the past few years, it would have been impossible to do so. And even if it had been produced, it could hardly have been adopted. Our experience has enabled us to answer new questions that arose under new circumstances. We have been stressing the need to uphold the Four Cardinal Principles, haven't we? We are truly upholding socialism. Otherwise, wouldn't we be "preferring socialist weeds to capitalist seedlings" as advocated by the Gang of Four? Veteran comrades must open their minds. I say the document is good because all the comrades on the Central Committee, the Central Advisory Commission and the Central Commission for Discipline Inspection agree with it and appreciate the necessity and importance of issuing such a programmatic document at this point. It is a good document.

"Decision" is in ten parts, all of which are important, but the ninth is the most important. The ninth part can be summed up "respecting knowledge and talented people". The key to success is to identify and employ talented people. To be more specific, some comrades now in their 50s are quite competent. But 10 years from now they will be in their 60s. We should be unhesitatingly promoting young and middle-aged cadres, especially those in their 30s and 40s, as suggested by Comrade Chen Yun. This is a good suggestion. Young people in this age group who are promoted can work longer. They may lack experience now but they will become experienced in a couple of years. They may be unqualified now but they will be qualified a couple of years from now. Their minds are more flexible. Next year Party consolidation will be conducted in units and enterprises at the grass-roots level. This is extremely important work, and its success will depend on finding a lot of capable young people. This is because by the end of the century, those now in their 30s will be only in their 40s and those in their 40s only in their 50s. But by the time we are fulfilling the second economic target, some of them will be getting along in years. We veteran comrades on the Advisory Commission should devote more attention to this problem. We must be open-minded about it, because otherwise nothing can be accomplished. We should persuade older comrades to vacate their leading posts. If they don't, there will be no positions for the young. Our general situation is one of stability and unity, but if there is a snag anywhere, it exists on this question. And we have not found satisfactory solutions yet. It doesn't matter much if problems crop up on other issues, but failure to solve this question will have serious consequences and will result in gross errors. It is not easy to ask middle-aged and older comrades to give up their posts. But that is what we have to do and we must not back down. I said two years ago that I hoped to be the first to retire. And I said that the Central Advisory Commission was a transitional measure to be replaced ultimately by a retirement system. We only have a limited number of posts; besides, we plan to streamline our administration. If the old do not vacate their posts, how can the young be promoted and if they can't, how can our cause thrive? In this respect also, we should learn from the developed countries. Some Third World countries are quite successful in solving this question. I was told recently that in a number of Third World countries most ministers are in their 30s. Some are older, but relatively few. Prime ministers are probably older but, in general, only in their 50s. We were young at the time of nationwide liberation. I was 45 and many comrades were even younger. I was 23 at the end of 1927 when I first served as Chief Secretary of the Central Committee. That was quite a high-ranking office. I didn't know much, but I managed. In short, choosing young cadres for promotion is an important responsibility of our Central Advisory Commission.

WE SHOULD FOLLOW OUR OWN ROAD BOTH IN REVOLUTION AND IN ECONOMIC DEVELOPMENT*

October 26, 1984

China is a major country as well as a minor one. When we say it is a major country, we mean it has a large population and a vast territory, and when we say it is a minor one, we mean it is still a relatively poor, developing country with a per capita GNP of only U.S. $300. So China is in fact both a minor and a major country. China is one of the permanent members of the Security Council of the United Nations. Its vote belongs firmly to the Third World, to the underdeveloped countries. We have said more than once that China belongs to the Third World. It will still belong to the Third World even in the future, after it is developed. China will never become a superpower.

China's economic development is now at a comparatively low level, which is not commensurate with its status as a country with such a large population and vast territory. Our achievements since the founding of the People's Republic are great. But our progress has been delayed by setbacks, notably the "cultural revolution"; things would be definitely different were it not for these setbacks. In the past five years we have broken with "Left" policies. We are now devoting ourselves

---

* Main points of a talk with President Maumoon Abdul Gayoom of the Republic of Maldives.

wholeheartedly to economic development. In these five years we have scored successes well beyond our expectations. It seems that we can achieve our goal of quadrupling the gross annual value of China's industrial and agricultural output and increasing per capita GNP to $800 by the end of the century. We need a peaceful international environment to ensure our development and the attainment of our great goal. We love peace.

Recently the Third Plenary Session of our Party's Twelfth Central Committee adopted the "Decision on Reform of the Economic Structure". The reform of the economic structure is now focused on the cities. Reform in the cities is more complicated than in the countryside. Some minor problems may arise in the process, but it doesn't matter. The correctness of the resolution adopted at the Plenary Session will be borne out in three to five years' time. Our economic development will be accelerated by adhering to the principles embraced in the decision.

If we have learned anything from our achievements in these years, it is that we were right to reaffirm the principle of seeking truth from facts advocated by Comrade Mao Zedong. The Chinese revolution owes its success to Comrade Mao Zedong, who blazed a Chinese road by integrating Marxism-Leninism with Chinese realities. In our present development programme we shall do likewise. It is precisely because, in accordance with this principle, we have been following our own road in these five years that our rural reforms have been successful. The recently adopted resolution on focusing our reform on the cities is another example of following our own road by integrating the fundamental principles of Marxism-Leninism with Chinese realities. The lesson we have learned from our setbacks is that this is what we must do. We may make mistakes in future. But first, we shall avoid big ones and second, we shall correct anything untoward as soon as it is discovered.

THE PRINCIPLES OF PEACEFUL COEXISTENCE HAVE A POTENTIALLY WIDE APPLICATION*

October 31, 1984

In opening to the outside world, China is not just opening to such developed countries as the United States, Japan and those in Western Europe. That is only one aspect of our policy. Another is South-South co-operation. A third is our opening to the Soviet Union and the East European countries. Altogether there are three major regions. There are many poor countries in the world. They all have special features of their own and the desire and possibility for development through co-operation. South-South co-operation is full of promise. There is much to be achieved.

There are two outstanding issues in the world today. One is the question of peace, the other the relationship between North and South. We find many other problems too, but none of them has the global, strategic, overall significance of these two. In the present-day world the North is developed and rich whereas the South is underdeveloped and poor. And relatively speaking, the rich are getting richer and the poor poorer. The South wants to change its state of poverty and backwardness, and the North needs a developed South. For where can the North find a market for its products if the South remains underdeveloped? The biggest problem facing

* Main points of a talk with President U San Yu of Burma.

the developed capitalist countries is the pace of their continued progress and development. In this connection, there is another side to South-South co-operation: it can promote North-South co-operation.

The Five Principles of Peaceful Coexistence provide the best way to handle the relations between nations.[12] Other ways—thinking in terms of "the socialist community", "bloc politics" or "spheres of influence", for example—lead to conflict, thus sharpening international tensions. Looking at the history of international relations we find that the Five Principles of Peaceful Coexistence have a potentially wide application.

Let us take the matter a step further. These principles would probably also help to solve a country's internal problems. The approach of "one country, two systems", which we have proposed in line with Chinese realities to reunify the nation, is likewise an embodiment of peaceful coexistence. To settle the Hongkong question, we are allowing Hongkong to keep its capitalist system unchanged for 50 years. The same principle holds true for Taiwan. And since Taiwan is different from Hongkong, it may also retain its army. In calling for the reunification of China on the basis of the "Three People's Principles", the Taiwan authorities, to say the least, lack a sense of reality. Is it possible to reunify the country by subjecting the mainland, with its billion people, to the current system in Taiwan with its population of a dozen million or so? Time and again we have advised the Taiwan authorities to abandon such thinking. A method should be devised by which neither side would swallow up the other. The one billion people on the mainland will continue to build socialism, while Taiwan may go on with its capitalism. Beijing will send no one to Taiwan. Wouldn't that be a case of peaceful coexistence? Therefore, the principles of peaceful coexistence provide a good solution not only to international issues, but to domestic problems as well.

The principles of peaceful coexistence can be applied to defuse explosive issues in international disputes. For instance, the question of Taiwan constitutes the main obstacle to better relations between China and the United States, and it is even possible that this question could develop into a crisis between the two nations. If the "one country, two systems" approach is adopted, not only would China be reunified, but the interests of the United States would not be impaired. There is a group of people in the United States today who, carrying on the "Dulles doctrine", regard Taiwan as a U.S. "aircraft carrier" or as a territory within the U.S. sphere of influence. Once the Taiwan question is solved through peaceful coexistence, the issue will be defused and these people will shed their illusions accordingly. This would be a very good thing for the peace and stability of the Pacific region and of the rest of the world.

THE ARMY SHOULD SUBORDINATE ITSELF TO THE GENERAL INTEREST, WHICH IS TO DEVELOP THE COUNTRY*

November 1, 1984

I am going to discuss the question of considering the general interest. By general interest I mean our national development. Our nation is full of vitality and is thriving in every sector. Even foreigners share this view and say so. This has been the situation for the last five years, and particularly for the last three years when our rural policies began to yield results. This increases our confidence. Why is it that we are now in a position to embark on reforms in the cities or, as we say, to dare "touch the tiger's backside"? I should say that the reforms are not without certain risks. A recent example was the run on consumer goods in Beijing. And it was not confined to Beijing, the same thing happened in many other cities too. We have foreseen all this. Why are we not afraid of it? Because we have quite a plentiful supply of consumer goods to fall back on, the sight of which reassures the people. The goal set by the Twelfth National Congress of the Party is to quadruple our annual industrial and agricultural product by the year 2000, a goal which, I can say with certainty, will be achieved. The targets set for major products in the

* Excerpt from a speech at a forum held by the Military Commission of the Central Committee of the Chinese Communist Party.

Sixth Five-Year Plan were met in the first three years, so that everything produced this year and next is a surplus. We planned a 6.5 per cent average annual growth rate during the first 10 years (1980-90) and a 7.2 per cent growth rate in 20 years. Now I can tell foreigners without hesitation that we shall meet this target. We used to say that it would take an immense effort on our part, and that is still true. But now we are in a position to say that we shall reach it. At the Plenary Session of the Central Advisory Commission, I said that this was a matter of utmost importance. Although our per capita GNP will not amount to much and will mean only a comparatively comfortable living standard, our country will become more powerful. So, it is doubly significant. A trillion U.S. dollars! That will be our national strength. Now, encouraged by the experience gained in rural reform, we have made up our minds to begin urban reform, or all-round reform. Of course, it will take us three to five years—three years in my opinion—before we can determine whether it will be successful.

On the one hand we shall open to the outside world, and on the other we shall invigorate our domestic economy. Reform means invigorating the economy. And doing that means opening up at home, or an aspect of the same policy. We are opening up in our relations with foreign countries and we are doing the same at home. Some of our people are not clear about the former, mistaking it for opening to the West only, when in fact we mean three regions. Yesterday, I had a talk with Burmese President U San Yu about the three regions. One is the developed countries in the West, which constitute our chief source of foreign funds and technology. The second is composed of the Soviet Union and the East European countries. Even though state-to-state relations are not normal, exchanges can go on, for instance, in commercial transactions, technology and even in joint ventures and technical innovations—innovations in the 156 projects [which were originally designed and built with the assistance of the Soviet Union], for example. They have a part to play in all these respects. The third region is the developing countries of the Third World, each of which has its special characteristics and strong points and offers enormous potentialities. Hence, opening to the outside world involves three regions, not just one. Invigorating our domestic economy and reforming our economic structure will proceed more rapidly than expected, which means a promising future. Some problems may crop up in the process. Never mind, there is nothing to be afraid of, because we shall move step by step, reviewing our work as we go, and try to correct promptly anything that goes wrong. However, there will be no fundamental changes, not with regard to our major policies.

What is essential now is that the Party, government, army and people throughout the land work wholeheartedly for national development, taking it into account in everything they do. The army has its role to play here. It must do nothing harmful to the general interest and all its work must conform to it and be governed by it. Since the development of all our armed services is tied to national development, they should devise ways to assist and actively participate in it. The air force, navy and the Commission in Charge of Science, Technology and Industry for National Defence should divert some of their resources to foster the development of the economy. For instance, the air force can spare some airports for civilian or both military and civilian use to help the state develop civil aviation. The navy can designate some of its ports for both military and civilian use and others for civilian use only, to help increase the handling capacity of the nation's ports. Our national defence industry, which is well equipped and has a huge contingent of technicians, should be put to full use in every aspect of national development in order to help boost civilian production. If these things are done, they can have only good results. In short, everyone should proceed from the general interest, always bear it in mind and help develop the economy by all possible means. A developed economy will make things easier for us. Once the general situation is improved and our national strength greatly increased, it will not be too difficult for us to produce a few more atom bombs, missiles and other pieces of modern equipment, whether for air, sea or land.

Another question is training people for both military and civilian jobs, which is also in the general interest. Our army has been doing a good job in this respect and has much to its credit. That's fine. The army trains these people in the interest of national development, and local authorities will warmly welcome the trainees. Such training will make it easier for demobilized cadres and soldiers to be transferred to civilian jobs. Comrade Yu Qiuli has told me that soldiers trained in raising pigs can readily find jobs.[13] And drivers are in great demand. The army has trained a large number of personnel with special technical skills, and transferring some of them to civilian trades and professions would provide support for local communities. So we should step up our work of training people for both military and civilian jobs.

I hope the comrades present here will encourage cadres at all levels to concern themselves with the general interest of the state, which is to develop our country over the next 20 years or, to be exact, the 16 years from now to the year 2000. In everything it does the army should subordinate itself to that general interest.

THE CONCEPT OF "ONE COUNTRY, TWO SYSTEMS" IS BASED ON CHINA'S REALITIES*

December 19, 1984

The leaders of our two countries have reached agreement on the question of Hongkong and have thus done something highly significant, something that will greatly benefit our countries and peoples. This problem has lasted for a century and a half. As long as it remained unsolved, it cast a shadow over the relations between us. Now that the shadow has been lifted, a bright prospect has opened up for co-operation between our two countries and friendly contact between our two peoples.

If the concept of "one country, two systems" has international significance, that should be attributed to Marxist dialectical materialism and historical materialism, or in the words of Chairman Mao Zedong, to the principle of seeking truth from facts. This concept was formulated on the basis of China's realities. The practical problem confronting China was how to settle the questions of Hongkong and Taiwan. There were two possible ways: one was peaceful, the other non-peaceful. To settle the Hongkong question peacefully, we had to take into consideration the actual conditions in Hongkong, China and Great Britain. In other words, the way in which we settled the question had to be acceptable to all three

* Excerpt from a talk with the British Prime Minister, Margaret Thatcher.

parties—to the people of China, of Britain and of Hongkong. If we had wanted to achieve reunification by imposing socialism on Hongkong, the Hongkong people would have rejected it and so would the British people. Reluctant acquiescence on their part would only have led to turmoil. Even if there had been no armed conflict, Hongkong would have become a bleak city with a host of problems, and that is not something we would have wanted. So the only solution to the Hongkong question that would be acceptable to all three parties was the "one country, two systems" arrangement, under which Hongkong would be allowed to retain its capitalist system and to maintain its status as a free port and a financial centre. There was no other alternative. The idea of "one country, two systems" had first been suggested not in connection with Hongkong but in connection with Taiwan. The nine principles proposed by Ye Jianying, Chairman of the Standing Committee of the National People's Congress, on the eve of National Day in 1981 were not summed up in the formula "one country, two systems", but that is in fact what they meant. And when the Hongkong question was put on the table two years ago, we presented the idea of "one country, two systems".

When this idea was put forward, it was considered a new formulation, one which had never been offered by our predecessors. Some people doubted that it would work. They will have to be answered by the facts. It seems to have worked so far. At least, the Chinese think so, because the negotiations of the past two years proved successful. This concept of "one country, two systems" has played a very important, if not decisive, role in the settlement of the Hongkong question. It has been accepted by all three parties. Its viability will be further proved 13 years from now and 50 years from now. Some people are worried whether China will abide by the agreement consistently. Your Excellency and the other British friends present here, and the people all over the world, may be sure that China will always keep its promise and believes that the "one country, two systems" proposition is viable.

A Japanese friend once asked me: Why do you specify a period of 50 years? Why do you need to keep Hongkong's current capitalist system unchanged for 50 years after 1997? What is the basis for this proposal? Do you have any particular reason in mind? I answered that we had, that the proposal was based on China's realities. China has set itself the ambitious goal of quadrupling the total value of its industrial and agricultural production in two decades—that is, by the end of this century—and of reaching a level of comparative prosperity. But even then, China will still not be a wealthy or developed country. So that is only our first ambitious goal. It will take another 30 to 50 years after that for China to become a truly developed country, to approach --not surpass—the developed countries. If we need to follow the policy of opening China to the rest of the world in this century, then 50 years later, when China is close to the level of the developed countries, we shall have even more reason to adhere to it. It would make no sense to depart from it. It is in China's vital interest to keep Hongkong prosperous and stable. When we gave the figure of 50 years, we were not speaking casually or on impulse but in consideration of the realities in China and our need for development. Similarly, we need a stable Taiwan during the end of this century and the first half of the next. Taiwan is an integral part of China. China can institute two systems within one and the same country. That is what we had in mind when we formulated our state policy. If people understand our fundamental viewpoint and the basis on which we have put forward this concept and established this policy, they will be convinced that the policy will not change. I also explained to the Japanese friend that if the open policy remains unchanged in the first half of the next century, it will be even less likely to change in the 50 years after that, because then China will have more economic exchanges with other countries and all countries will be more mutually dependent and inseparable.

I should also like to ask the Prime Minister to make it clear to the people of Hongkong and of the rest of the world that the concept of "one country, two systems" includes not only capitalism but also socialism, which will be firmly maintained on the mainland of China, where one billion people live. There are one billion people on the mainland, approximately 20 million on Taiwan and 5.5 million in Hongkong. A problem arises of how to handle relations between such widely divergent numbers. Since one billion people, the overwhelming majority, live under socialism in a vast area, we can afford to allow capitalism in these small, limited areas at our side. If this were not the case, capitalism might swallow up socialism. We believe the existence of capitalism in a limited area will actually be conducive to the development of socialism. By the same token, we have opened some 20 cities to the outside world, on condition that the socialist economy is dominant there. We are not afraid that they might change the nature of our socialist economy. On the contrary, the policy of opening to the outside world favours the growth of the socialist economy.

PEACE AND DEVELOPMENT ARE THE TWO OUTSTANDING ISSUES IN THE WORLD TODAY*

March 4, 1985

Different people may have different attitudes towards the development of China. They analyse this question from different standpoints, depending on whether they think China's development will or will not be in their own interest. I have been thinking about this too. I should like to discuss this question from two points of view, one political, the other economic.

From the political point of view, there is one thing that I can state positively, and that is that China seeks to preserve world peace and stability, not to destroy them. The stronger China grows, the better the chances are for preserving world peace. Some people used to regard China—that is, the People's Republic—as a "warlike" country. In reply to that view, not only I but also other Chinese leaders, including the late Chairman Mao Zedong and Premier Zhou Enlai, stated on many occasions that China desires peace more than anything else. In the days when Chairman Mao Zedong and Premier Zhou Enlai were leading the country, China was already opposed to superpower hegemony, regarding it as the source of war, by which we meant not local war but potential world war. Only the two superpowers have the capacity to initiate

---

* Excerpt from a talk with a delegation from the Japanese Chamber of Commerce and Industry.

world war, while the other countries, such as China, Japan and the European countries, are not in a position to do so. It follows that opposing superpower hegemony means preserving world peace. Since the downfall of the Gang of Four, we too have made it a state policy to oppose superpower hegemony and keep world peace.

Generally speaking, the forces for world peace are growing, but the danger of war still exists. Not much progress has been made in the talks on control of nuclear arms and of weapons in outer space. That's why for many years we have been emphasizing the danger of war. However, there have been some changes in our views. We now think that although there is still the danger of war, the forces that can deter it are growing, and we find that encouraging. The Japanese people do not want war, nor do the people of Europe. The Third World countries, including China, hope for national development, and war will bring them nothing good. The growing strength of the Third World—and of the most populous country, China, in particular—is an important factor for world peace. So from the political point of view, a stronger China will help promote peace and stability in the Asian and Pacific regions and in the rest of the world as well. Some people are talking about the international situation in terms of a big triangle. Frankly, the China angle is not strong enough. China is both a major country and a minor one. When we say it is a major country, we mean it has a large population and a vast territory, although it has more mountains than arable land. But at the same time, China is a minor country, an underdeveloped or developing country. It is a minor one in terms of its ability to safeguard peace and deter war. When China is fully developed, that ability will be greatly enhanced. I can say with certainty that by the end of the century China will have quadrupled the total annual value of its industrial and agricultural production and reached a level of comparative prosperity, as I once told Mr. Masayoshi Ohira. When that time comes, China will surely play a bigger role in maintaining world peace and stability.

From the economic point of view, the two really great issues confronting the world today, issues of global strategic significance, are: first, peace, and second, economic development. The first involves East-West relations, while the second involves North-South relations. In short, countries in the East, West, North and South are all involved, but the North-South relations are the key question. What problems will the developed countries, such as Japan and the countries in Europe and North America, be faced with in their continued development? You will have to seek outlets for your capital and expand your trade and markets. Unless these problems are solved, the growth of the developed countries can only be very limited in the long run. I have discussed this question with many Japanese friends and also with friends from Europe and the United States. They have been preoccupied with it too. There are more than 4 billion people in the world today, about three quarters of whom live in the Third World. The other quarter—about 1.1 or 1.2 billion—live in the developed countries, including the Soviet Union, countries in Eastern Europe (which cannot be regarded as fully developed), in Western Europe and in North America, and Japan, Australia and New Zealand. It is not likely that these developed nations, with a combined population of only 1.1 or 1.2 billion, can continue to grow while the developing countries, with a combined population of more than 3 billion, remain in poverty. Of course, some Third World countries are becoming more prosperous, but they cannot yet be considered developed. And many others are still extremely poor. Unless their economic problems are solved, it will be hard for all the

Third World countries to develop and for the developed countries to advance further. The total volume of foreign trade of even so large a country as China was only $50 billion last year. If China could double that figure, making it $100 billion, the world market would be expanded, wouldn't it? If China could quadruple that figure, making it $200 billion, it would have even more exchanges with other countries. Foreign trade involves both import and export. With a quadrupled volume of foreign trade China would be able to absorb more foreign capital and products. Some developed countries are worried that if China were fully developed and expanded its exports, that would adversely affect their own exports. I agree that it would create competition. But with all their advanced technology and first-rate products, what do the developed countries have to fear? In short, if the countries in the South are not duly developed, the countries in the North will find only very limited outlets for their capital and products; indeed, if the South remains poor, the North will find no outlets at all.

So, I think the decision of Japanese enterprises to take a positive attitude towards economic and technological cooperation with China is of strategic importance.

UNITY DEPENDS ON IDEALS AND DISCIPLINE*

March 7, 1985

The domestic situation is excellent at present. Still, I'd like to call your attention to one point: while building a socialist society with Chinese characteristics, we must continue to promote not only material progress but also cultural and ideological progress. We must uphold the principle of the "five things to emphasize", "four things to beautify" and "three things to love"[14] and encourage all our people to have lofty ideals and moral integrity, to become better educated and to cultivate a strong sense of discipline. Of these, lofty ideals and a strong sense of discipline are the most important. We must constantly urge our people, young people in particular, to have high ideals. How was it that we were able to survive untold hardships, overcome the most difficult and dangerous conditions and bring the revolution to victory? It was precisely because we had ideals and a belief in Marxism and communism. Now we are building socialism, and our ultimate goal is to realize communism. I hope people doing propaganda work will never lose sight of that. Our modernization programme is a socialist programme, not anything else. All our policies for carrying out reform, opening to the

---

* Impromptu remarks at the National Conference on Scientific and Technological Work, made after delivering a speech entitled "The Reform of the Science and Technology Management System Is Designed to Liberate the Productive Forces".

outside world and invigorating the domestic economy are designed to develop the socialist economy. We allow the development of individual economy, of joint ventures with both Chinese and foreign investment and of enterprises wholly owned by foreign businessmen, but socialist public ownership will always remain predominant. The aim of socialism is to make all our people prosperous, not to create polarization. If our policies led to polarization, it would mean that we had failed; if a new bourgeoisie emerged, it would mean that we had strayed from the right path. In encouraging some regions to become prosperous first, we intend that they should help the economically backward ones to develop. Similarly, in encouraging some people to become prosperous first, we intend that they should help others who are still in poverty to become better off, so that there will be common prosperity rather than polarization. A limit should be placed on the wealth of people who become prosperous first, through the income tax, for example. In addition, we should encourage them to contribute money to run schools and build roads, although we definitely shouldn't set quotas for them. We should encourage these people to make donations, but it's better not to give such donations too much publicity.

In short, predominance of public ownership and common prosperity are the two fundamental socialist principles that we must adhere to. We shall firmly put them into practice. And ultimately we shall move on to communism. Some people are worried that China might go capitalist. We cannot say that their concern is entirely without reason. We shall use facts, not empty words, to dispel their anxieties and to answer the people who, on the contrary, hope we will go capitalist. The press, television and all other mass media must pay attention to this work. We ourselves are imbued with communist ideals and convictions. We must make a point of fostering those ideals and convictions in the next or next two generations. We must see to it that our young people do not fall captive to decadent capitalist ideas. We must make absolutely sure of that.

Ideals cannot be realized without discipline. Discipline and freedom form a unity of opposites; both are indispensable. How can a vast country like China be united and organized? Through ideals and discipline. Strength comes from organization. Without ideals and discipline our country would be only a heap of loose sand, as it was in the old days. How, then, could we make a success of revolution and construction? At present there are certain phenomena that demand our attention. For example, there is a lack of ideals, as is manifested in the tendency to put money above everything else. It goes without saying that this sort of thing should be subjected to appropriate criticism, but first of all we have to recognize that the problem really exists. Some institutions have established companies, doing business with funds allocated by the state. And there are other kinds of dishonest practices that the masses are indignant about. We should remind people, especially Party members, that it is wrong to do these things. Aren't we in the midst of a Party rectification movement? We should give first priority to eliminating these bad practices.

During the current economic reform some tricky practices have appeared. There are people who say, "You have your policies, and I have my ways of getting around them." Indeed, they have plenty of ways. Party members must strictly observe Party discipline. Everybody, whether a member of the Party or not, must abide by the laws of the state. Abiding by the laws of the state is included in Party discipline. The highest criterion of discipline is whether one truly safeguards and implements the policies of the Party and the state. Ideals and discipline, then, are the two things we must never forget. We should make it clear to the people, including our children, that we uphold socialism and communism and that the purpose of our policies in every field is to advance the socialist cause and eventually to realize communism.

EXPAND POLITICAL DEMOCRACY AND CARRY OUT ECONOMIC REFORM*

April 15, 1985

When you visited China in 1973, there was great unrest because of the "cultural revolution", which was still going on, although nearing its end. At that time the "Left" ideology was predominant in our society. As a consequence social and economic development was very slow.

Let me give you an outline of the history of new China.

After the founding of the People's Republic, in the rural areas we initiated agrarian reform[15] and launched a movement for the co-operative transformation of agriculture,[16] while in the cities we conducted the socialist transformation of capitalist industry and commerce.[17] We were successful in both. However, from 1957 on, China was plagued by "Left" ideology, which gradually became dominant. During the Great Leap Forward in 1958,[18] people rushed headlong into mass action to establish people's communes. They placed lopsided emphasis on making the communes large in size and collective in nature, urging everyone to "eat from the same big pot", and by so doing brought disaster upon the nation. We won't even mention the "cultural revolution". For most of the period from 1976, when the Gang of Four was smashed, to 1978, we didn't know what to do and kept repeating "Left" mistakes. During the 20 years from 1958 to

---

* Main points of a talk with Vice-President Ali Hassan Mwinyi of the United Republic of Tanzania.

1978 the income of peasants and workers rose only a little, and consequently their standard of living remained very low. The development of the productive forces was sluggish during those years. In 1978 per capita GNP was less than $250. In December 1978, when the Eleventh Central Committee of the Communist Party convened its Third Plenary Session, we made a sober analysis of China's realities and summed up our experience. We reaffirmed the great achievements scored in the 30 years from the founding of new China in 1949 through 1978, but that didn't mean that everything we had done was successful. The socialist system we have established is a good one and we must adhere to it. The realization of socialism and communism was the ultimate goal and lofty ideal we Marxists set for ourselves during the revolutionary years. Now that we are trying to reform the economy, we shall continue to keep to the socialist road and to uphold the ideal of communism. This is something our younger generation in particular must understand. But the problem is: What is socialism? What are its characteristics? These questions are being raised, and we have to answer them.

Comrade Mao Zedong was a great leader, and it was under his leadership that the Chinese revolution triumphed. But he made the grave mistake of neglecting the development of the productive forces. I do not mean he didn't want to develop them. The point is, not all of the methods he used were correct. For instance, the people's communes were established in defiance of the laws governing socio-economic development. The most important lesson we have learned, among a great many others, is that we must be clear about what socialism is and how to build it.

The fundamental principle of Marxism is that the productive forces must be developed. The goal for Marxists is to realize communism, which must be built on the basis of highly developed productive forces. What is a communist society? It is a society in which there is vast material wealth and in which the principle of from each according to his ability, to each according to his needs is applied. That principle cannot be applied without highly developed productive forces and highly advanced science and technology. According to Marxism, socialism constitutes the first stage of communism and will last for a long historical period. The primary task in the socialist period is to develop the productive forces and gradually improve people's material and cultural life. Our experience in the 20 years from 1958 to 1978 teaches us that poverty is not socialism, that socialism means eliminating poverty. Unless you are developing the productive forces and raising people's living standards, you cannot say that you are building socialism.

At the Third Plenary Session of the Eleventh Central Committee our Party, having summed up our experience, laid down a series of new policies. There were two major domestic ones: to expand political democracy and to carry out economic reform and corresponding social reforms. Our foreign policy is to oppose hegemonism and preserve world peace. Peace is the prime objective of our foreign policy. People all over the world are demanding peace and we too need peace for national construction. Without a peaceful environment, how much construction could there be?

After the Third Plenary Session we proceeded to explore ways of building socialism in China. Finally we decided to develop the productive forces and gradually expand the economy. The first goal we set was to achieve comparative prosperity by the end of the century. We could not go beyond the realities and set too ambitious a goal, because at the end of 1979, when we made this decision, we had only two decades left until the end of the century. So taking population increase into consideration, we planned to quadruple our GNP, which meant that per capita GNP would grow from $250 to $800 or $1,000. We shall lead a much better life when we reach this level, although it is still much lower than that of the developed countries. That is why we call it comparative prosperity. When we attain that level, China's GNP will have reached $1,000 billion, representing increased national strength. And the most populous nation in the world will have shaken off poverty and be able to make a greater contribution to mankind. With a GNP of $1,000 billion as a springboard, within 30 or 50 more years—50, to be more accurate—China may reach its second goal, to approach the level of the developed countries. How are we to go about achieving these goals? We must observe the laws governing social development. We have decided to follow an open policy both internationally and domestically. It is very important to open to the outside world. No country can develop in isolation, with its doors closed. It would be impossible for China to achieve its first and second goals if it didn't open its doors to other countries, increase international contacts, introduce advanced methods, science and technology from developed countries and use their capital. Keeping its doors closed won't work. That is what we mean by pursuing an open policy internationally. Pursuing an open policy domestically means carrying out reform. The reform we are undertaking is a comprehensive one, including not only the economy but also education and all other fields of endeavour. We began our reform in the countryside. The main point of the rural reform has been to bring the peasants' initiative into full play by introducing the responsibility system and discarding the system whereby everybody ate from the same big pot. Why did we start in the countryside? Because that is where 80 per cent of China's population lives. If we didn't raise living standards in the countryside, the society would be unstable. Industry, commerce and other sectors of the economy cannot develop on the basis of the poverty of 80 per cent of the population. After three years of practice the rural reform has proved successful. I can say with assurance it is a good policy. The countryside has assumed a new look. The living standards of 90 per cent of the rural population have been raised. Those of the remaining 10 per cent are still low, but it should not be too difficult to solve that problem. Just now you mentioned that you had seen many new tall buildings in Beijing, but they aren't the big changes in China. The big changes in China are to be found in the countryside, where the standard of living of 90 per cent of the inhabitants has been raised.

After our success in rural reform we embarked on urban reform. Urban reform is more complicated and risky. This is especially true in China, because we have no experience in this regard. Also, China has traditionally been a very closed society, so that people lack information about what's going on elsewhere. That is one of our major weaknesses. Every step, every measure we take in urban reform will affect tens of thousands of families. However, we are fully aware of the risks and shall proceed carefully, drawing on the successful experience of rural reform to help us avoid major mistakes. Of course, minor and even not-so-minor mistakes are unavoidable. As Premier Zhao Ziyang has told you, when the urban reform began, we issued too much currency, which made commodity prices unstable. And other sorts of problems may arise in future because of our lack of experience. The principle we have laid down for ourselves is that we must be both determined and on the alert. By determined we mean that we must carry out the reform unswervingly; by on the alert we mean that we must promptly correct all mistakes as soon as they are identified. Reform is what the people want and demand. Although some problems have arisen in the process, we are confident that we can handle them. If it took us three years to complete the rural reform, we can expect that it will be three to five years before we can judge the success of the urban reform. We are sure it will be successful. To make it so we certainly won't rely on the help of God, we shall rely on our own efforts, learning from experience and pushing resolutely ahead. We are doing something that China has never done before, not in thousands of years. The current reform will have an impact not only domestically but also internationally.

So, that is a brief history of new China and of what we have done in recent years.

How can people build socialism? You said you wanted to learn from China's experience. The road to socialism in China has been full of twists and turns. But the experience of the last 20 years has taught us one very important principle: To build socialism we must adhere to Marxist dialectical materialism and historical materialism or, in Comrade Mao Zedong's words, in everything we do we must seek truth from facts and proceed from reality.

INCREASE ECONOMIC TIES WITH EUROPE*

April 18, 1985

As China's economy grows, its foreign trade will increase. Europe should have an appropriate share in our foreign trade. I want to mention two points in this connection. One is technology transfer. European countries are comparatively liberal in this respect—compared to others, that is. The other point is that both sides should explore trade channels. Trade is always a two-way matter, in this case with China importing European products and European countries purchasing Chinese products. China won't buy foreign products if it can't afford them. When China's economy expands thanks to your technological assistance, its foreign trade will expand accordingly. At present China's annual volume of trade is $50 billion and will be $100 billion if doubled. If it is quadrupled by the end of the century, it will be $200 billion. That is not a large sum in the eyes of developed countries, but it would be an enormous increase for China. Trade with Europe accounts for only a small proportion of our foreign trade. If it makes up a larger proportion in future, we shall be very pleased. For the past three years we have been considering how to increase economic ties with Europe. That's our policy. I hope European entrepreneurs will continue to create condi-

---

* Excerpt from a talk with the former British Prime Minister, Edward Heath.

tions for more of China's commodities to enter the European market.

BOURGEOIS LIBERALIZATION MEANS TAKING THE CAPITALIST ROAD*

May and June 1985

I

The mainland will continue on its socialist road and not turn off onto the evil road to capitalism. One of the distinguishing features of socialism is that the wealth created belongs first to the state and second to the people; it is therefore impossible for a new bourgeoisie to emerge. By the end of this century, our per capita GNP will have reached $800. Part of that amount will go to the state, which will spend it for the benefit of the people on education, scientific research and, to a lesser degree, national defence. The bulk of this average GNP will go to raise the people's living standards and educational level. Socialism is different from capitalism in that it means common prosperity, not polarization of income.

Since the defeat of the Gang of Four an ideological trend has appeared that we call bourgeois liberalization. Its exponents worship the "democracy" and "freedom" of the Western capitalist countries and reject socialism. This cannot be allowed. China must modernize; it must absolutely not liber-

---

* Excerpts from, respectively, a talk with Prof. Chen Ku-ying, formerly of Taiwan University, on May 20, 1985, and a talk with the committee chairmen of a symposium on the question of the mainland and Taiwan on June 6, 1985.

alize or take the capitalist road as countries of the West have done. Those exponents of bourgeois liberalization who have violated state law must be dealt with severely. Because what they are doing is, precisely, "speaking out freely, airing their views fully, putting up big-character posters" and producing illegal publications—all of which only creates unrest and brings back the practices of the "cultural revolution". We must keep this evil trend in check. Without ideals and a strong sense of discipline it would be impossible for China to adhere to the socialist system, to develop the socialist economy and to realize the modernization programme. And it would likewise be impossible for it to proceed with socialist construction in an environment of political unrest and instability.

At the Third Plenary Session of the Eleventh Central Committee the Party decided on the policy of opening to the outside world and at the same time demanded a curb on bourgeois liberalization. These two things are related. Unless we curb bourgeois liberalization, we cannot put our open policy into effect. Liberal thinking still exists, not only in the society at large but also inside the Party. Our modernization drive and the open policy must exclude bourgeois liberalization, because once this trend is allowed to spread, it will undermine our cause. In short, our goal is to create a stable political environment; otherwise, we can accomplish nothing. Our major task is to build up the country, and less important things should be subordinated to it. Even if there is a good reason for having them, the major task must take precedence.

In 1980 the National People's Congress adopted a special resolution to delete from Article 45 of the Constitution the provision that citizens "have the right to speak out freely, air their views fully, hold great debates and write big-character posters". Those who worship Western "democracy" are always insisting on those rights. But having gone through the bitter experience of the ten-year "cultural revolution", China cannot restore them.

II

Several persons who have advocated bourgeois liberalization and violated state law have been dealt with according to law. In China, bourgeois liberalization means taking the capitalist road and leads to disunity. I'm not talking about the reunification of Taiwan with the mainland now but about unity on the mainland. Bourgeois liberalization would plunge our society into turmoil and make it impossible for us to proceed with the work of construction. To check bourgeois liberalization is therefore a matter of principle and one of key importance for us.

Your view of the way we dealt with these few persons is different from ours. That's because you think of this question merely in terms of human rights. What are human rights? How many people enjoy them? Do those rights belong to the majority, to the minority or to all the people in a country? Our concept of human rights is different from that of the Western world, because we see the question from a different point of view.

CONCRETE ACTIONS FOR THE MAINTENANCE OF WORLD PEACE*

June 4, 1985

The danger of world war still exists. Because of the arms race between the two superpowers, the factors making for war will increase. But the people want peace and oppose war, so the world forces for peace are growing faster than the forces for war. The Chinese government will always stand by its policy of opposing hegemonism and safeguarding world peace, pursue an independent foreign policy and side firmly with the forces in favour of peace. As long as the forces for peace continue to expand, it is possible that world war will not break out for a fairly long time to come, and there is hope of maintaining world peace.

China must concentrate on economic development if it wants to become a modern, powerful socialist country. Therefore we need a peaceful international environment and are striving to create and maintain one. Economic development is our primary objective, and everything else must be subordinated to it.

Our government has decided to reduce the People's Liberation Army by one million men. This troop reduction bears witness to the strength and confidence of the Chinese government and the Chinese people. It shows that the People's

* Excerpt from a speech at an enlarged meeting of the Military Commission of the Central Committee of the Chinese Communist Party.

Republic of China, with a population of one billion, is willing to take concrete actions to help maintain world peace.

THE SPECIAL ECONOMIC ZONES SHOULD SHIFT THEIR ECONOMY FROM A DOMESTIC ORIENTATION TO AN EXTERNAL ORIENTATION*

August 1, 1985

We have only just begun to shift the economy of our special economic zones from a domestic orientation to an external orientation, and so we still don't have many good, exportable products. Until Shenzhen has become a city with an export-oriented economy, it cannot be truly considered a special economic zone, and it cannot be said to be developing properly. But I understand there has been some progress in this direction.

Recently I told a foreign guest that the Shenzhen Special Economic Zone was an experiment. Some people abroad reacted to this with suspicion. They wondered if China was going to change its policies again, if I had reversed my previous judgement and changed my mind about the establishment of special economic zones. So I want to confirm two things here and now. First, the policy of establishing special economic zones is correct; and second, the Shenzhen Special Economic Zone is an experiment. There is no contradiction here. Our entire policy of opening to the outside world is an experiment too, and a big one from the world point of view.

---

* Excerpt from a talk with the 13th delegation sent to China by the Komei Party of Japan.

In short, China's policy of opening to the outside world will remain unchanged, but in pursuing it we must proceed with caution. We have achieved some successes, but we must stay modest.

REFORM IS THE ONLY WAY FOR CHINA TO DEVELOP ITS PRODUCTIVE FORCES*

August 28, 1985

We did a great deal of work between 1949, when the People's Republic of China was founded, and 1976, when Chairman Mao Zedong passed away. We were particularly successful during the period of transition from new-democratic revolution to socialist revolution, in which we carried out agrarian reform and completed the socialist transformation of agriculture, handicrafts and capitalist industry and commerce. We began to experience some trouble in 1957, when "Left" ideology appeared. It was necessary for us to combat bourgeois Rightists,[19] but we went too far. The spread of "Left" thinking led to the Great Leap Forward in 1958. That was a serious mistake. Disregarding objective conditions, we urged our people to go all out for making steel. This, together with a series of other "Left" policies, resulted in great suffering. During the three years of economic difficulty from 1959 through 1961, industrial and agricultural output dropped, so that commodities were in short supply. The people didn't have enough to eat, and their enthusiasm was greatly dampened. At that time our Party and Chairman Mao Zedong enjoyed high prestige, and we explained to the people frankly why the situation was so difficult. We aban-

---

* Excerpt from a talk with Robert Mugabe, Prime Minister of Zimbabwe and President of the Zimbabwe African National Union (Patriotic Front).

doned the slogan of the Great Leap Forward and adopted more realistic policies instead. It took us three years to recover. But our guiding ideology still contained remnants of "Left" thinking. The year 1962 saw the beginnings of recovery, and in 1963 and 1964 things were looking up. But once again "Left" thinking came to the fore. In 1965 it was said that certain persons who were in power in the Party were taking the capitalist road. Then came the "cultural revolution", in which the "Left" ideology was carried to its extreme. The "cultural revolution" actually began in 1965, but it was officially declared only a year later. It lasted a whole decade, from 1966 through 1976, during which time almost all the veteran cadres who formed the backbone of the Party were brought down. It was they who were made the targets of the "cultural revolution". That is what we call the ultra-Left trend of thought.

After the downfall of the Gang of Four, we began to set things to rights, that is, to correct the ultra-Left trend of thought. But we still maintained that it was necessary to uphold Marxism-Leninism and Mao Zedong Thought. When we met in 1981, I talked about keeping to the socialist road, upholding the people's democratic dictatorship, upholding leadership by the Communist Party, and upholding Marxism-Leninism and Mao Zedong Thought. Now we call these the Four Cardinal Principles. If we do not uphold them in our effort to correct ultra-Left thinking, we shall end up "correcting" Marxism-Leninism and socialism.

We summed up our experience in building socialism in the past few decades. We had not been quite clear about what socialism is. What is the essence of Marxism? Another term for Marxism is communism. It is for the realization of communism that we have struggled for so many years. We believe in communism, and our ideal is to bring it into being.

In our darkest days we were sustained by the ideal of communism. It was for the realization of this ideal that countless people laid down their lives. What is a communist society? It is one in which there is no exploitation of man by man, there is great material abundance and the principle of from each according to his ability, to each according to his needs is applied. It is impossible to apply that principle without overwhelming material wealth. In order to realize communism, we have to accomplish the tasks set in the socialist stage. They are legion, but the fundamental one is to develop the productive forces so as to provide the material basis for communism. Socialism, whose ultimate aim is the realization of communism, should develop the productive forces and then demonstrate its superiority over capitalism. For a long time we neglected the development of the socialist productive forces. From 1957 on they grew at a snail's pace. In that year the peasants' average annual net income was about 70 yuan, which meant that they were very poor. That figure was about the same as what a factory worker earned in a month. In 1966, when the "cultural revolution" was launched, the peasants' annual net income rose only very slightly. Although peasants in some areas were better off, those in many other areas could barely manage to live from hand to mouth. Of course, even that was progress, compared with the old days. Still, it was far from a socialist standard of living. During the "cultural revolution" things went from bad to worse.

By setting things to rights, we mean developing the productive forces while upholding the Four Cardinal Principles. To develop the productive forces, we have to reform the economic structure and open to the outside world. It is in order to assist the growth of the socialist productive forces that we absorb capital from capitalist countries and introduce their technology. After the Third Plenary Session of the

Eleventh Central Committee we began our reform step by step, starting with the countryside. The rural reform has achieved good results, and there has been a noticeable change in the countryside. Drawing on our successful experience in rural reform, we embarked on urban reform. Urban reform, a comprehensive undertaking involving all sectors, has been going on for a year now, ever since the second half of last year. Since it is much more complicated than rural economic reform, mistakes and risks are unavoidable, and that's something we are quite aware of. But economic reform is the only way to develop the productive forces. We have full confidence in urban reform, although it will take from three to five years to demonstrate the correctness of our policies.

In the course of reform it is very important for us to maintain our socialist orientation. We are trying to achieve modernization in industry, agriculture, national defence and science and technology. But in front of the word "modernization" is a modifier, "socialist", making it the "four socialist modernizations". The policies of invigorating our domestic economy and opening to the outside world are being carried out in accordance with the principles of socialism. Socialism has two major requirements. First, its economy must be dominated by public ownership, which may consist of both ownership by the entire people and ownership by the collective. Our publicly owned economy accounts for more than 90 per cent of the total. At the same time, we allow a small proportion of individual economy to develop, we absorb foreign capital and introduce advanced technology, and we even encourage foreign enterprises to establish factories in China. All that will serve as a supplement to the socialist economy based on public ownership; it cannot and will not undermine it. While half of the investment in a joint venture comes from abroad, the other half comes from the socialist sector, which will therefore also benefit from the growth of the enterprise. Half of its profits go to the socialist sector, and the state collects taxes on all of them. An even more important aspect of joint ventures is that from them we can learn managerial skills and advanced technology that will help us to develop our socialist economy. We are also happy to have foreign businessmen launch wholly foreign-owned enterprises, on which we can also levy taxes and from which we can also learn technical and managerial skills. They will bring no harm to socialist ownership. As of now, there has been only limited foreign investment, far less than we feel we need. The second requirement of socialism is that there must be no polarization of rich and poor. If there is, the reform will have been a failure. We have given much thought to this question in the course of formulating and implementing our policies. Is it possible that a new bourgeoisie will emerge? A handful of bourgeois elements may appear, but they will not form a class. There will be no harm so long as we keep our socialist public ownership predominant, and so long as we guard against polarization. In the last four years we have been proceeding along these lines. In short, we must keep to socialism.

Let me add that when we talk about the open policy, we should be sure not to overlook the role played by the state apparatus. Our socialist state apparatus is so powerful that it can intervene to correct any deviations. To be sure, the open policy entails risks. Some decadent bourgeois things may be brought into China. But with our socialist policies and state apparatus, we shall be able to cope with them. So there is nothing to fear. Our comrades have published a collection of some of my speeches, entitled *Build Socialism with Chinese Characteristics*, which includes, for instance, my opening speech at the Twelfth National Party Congress. I don't know if you have read it.

We were victorious in the Chinese revolution precisely because we applied the universal principles of Marxism-Leninism to our own realities. In building socialism we have had both positive and negative experiences, and they are equally useful to us. I hope you will particularly study our "Left" errors. History bears witness to the losses we have suffered on account of those errors. Being totally dedicated to the revolution, we are liable to be too impetuous. It is true that we have good intentions, that we are eager to see the realization of communism at an early date. But often our very eagerness has prevented us from making a sober analysis of subjective and objective conditions, and we have therefore acted in contradiction to the laws governing the development of the objective world. In the past China made the mistake of trying to plunge ahead too fast. We hope you will give special consideration to our negative experiences. Of course one can learn from the experience of other countries, but one must never copy everything they have done.

SPEECH AT THE NATIONAL CONFERENCE OF THE COMMUNIST PARTY OF CHINA

September 23, 1985

Comrades,

This National Conference has been a very good one. It has successfully accomplished the scheduled tasks. Now I shall speak on four points.

First, about the general situation and the reform.

As is clear to everyone, the period of almost seven years since the Third Plenary Session of the Eleventh Central Committee has been a crucial one and one of the best since the founding of the People's Republic. It has not been easy to make it so. We have done mainly two things: we have set wrong things right, and we have launched the comprehensive reform.

For many years we suffered badly from one major error: after the socialist transformation of the ownership of the means of production had been basically accomplished, we still took class struggle as the key link and neglected to develop the productive forces. The "cultural revolution" carried this tendency to the extreme. Since the Third Plenary Session of the Eleventh Central Committee, the Party has shifted the focus of all its work to the drive for socialist modernization and, while adhering to the Four Cardinal Principles, has concentrated on developing the productive forces. That was the most important thing we did to set things right. The good situation we have today would not have come about if we had not thoroughly corrected the "Left" mistakes and resolutely shifted the focus of our work. At the same time, if we had not conscientiously adhered to the four principles, we would not have been able to maintain political stability and unity, and we would even have gone from correcting "Left" mistakes to "correcting" socialism and Marxism-Leninism. And then the good situation we have today would not have come about either.

The issue of reform was already raised at the Third Plenary Session of the Eleventh Central Committee. When the reform first started in the countryside, people said all sorts of things about it. But after three years, when many problems that had arisen in practice had been solved and good results had been achieved, there was more agreement about it. Of course new problems will crop up and have to be tackled. Since the Third Plenary Session of the Twelfth Central Committee, reform has focused on the cities. After years of preparation, and on the basis of the success of the reform in the rural areas, we have gradually undertaken a comprehensive reform of the economic structure. The reform has stimulated the development of the productive forces and has resulted in a series of profound changes in economic life, social life, people's work style and their mentality. This reform is part of the self-perfecting process of the socialist system, and in certain areas and to a certain extent it is also a revolutionary change. It is a major undertaking that shows we have begun to find a way of building socialism with Chinese characteristics.

In the reform we have consistently followed two fundamental principles. One is the predominance of the socialist public sector of the economy; the other is common prosperity. The utilization of foreign investment capital in a planned way and the promotion of a degree of individual economy are both serving the development of the socialist economy as a whole. It is precisely for the purpose of enabling more and more people to become prosperous until all are prosperous that some areas and some people are encouraged to do so first. The standard of living of most people, with a few exceptions, has improved to varying degrees. Naturally, some negative phenomena are bound to appear in the process of reform. As long as we face them squarely and take firm steps to deal with them, it will not be difficult to solve these problems.

The all-round reform of our economic structure has just begun. The general orientation and principles are already established, but we still have to work out specific rules and regulations by trial and error. While identifying and tackling problems early, we must seize the opportunity of the moment and vigorously explore new possibilities, striving to complete the reform in the not-too-distant future. It is my belief that no matter how many difficulties may arise, all things that are in the fundamental interest of the vast majority of the people and are supported by the masses will succeed.

Second, about the Seventh Five-Year Plan.

The Proposal for the Seventh Five-Year Plan, which has been adopted by this Conference, is a good document setting forth correct principles and policies and realistic targets.

It is projected that during the period of the Plan the annual growth rate of the total value of industrial and agricultural production will be about 7 per cent, a figure on which the Standing Committee of the Political Bureau has unanimously agreed, and which may be exceeded in practice. That growth rate cannot be considered low. If the growth rate were too high, it would create many problems that would have a negative effect on the reform and on social conduct. It is better to be prudent. We must control the scale of investment in fixed assets and see that capital construction is not over-extended. To guarantee the planned growth rate, we must manage production well, ensure quality, and seek economic and social returns.

The period of the Seventh Five-Year Plan is a very important one. If at the end of these five years the reform has been basically completed and the economy is developing in a sound, steady, balanced way, then we are sure to meet the targets set by the Twelfth Party Congress for the end of the century.

People are saying that notable changes have taken place in China. I said to some foreign guests recently that these were only small changes. When we have quadrupled the gross value of our annual industrial and agricultural production and are comparatively prosperous, we can say there have been changes of medium importance. By the middle of the next century, when we approach the level of the advanced countries, then there will have been really great changes. At that time the strength of China and its role in the world will be quite different. We shall be able to make greater contributions to mankind.

Third, about a socialist society with advanced culture and ideology.

The question of building a socialist society that is culturally and ideologically advanced was raised long ago. The central and local authorities and the army have done a great deal of work in this regard. In particular, a large number of advanced persons have emerged from among the masses, and that has had a very favourable impact on society. However, considering the country as a whole, we must admit that so far the results of our work are not very satisfactory, mainly because it has not had the serious attention of the entire Party membership. We exert ourselves for socialism not only because socialism provides conditions for faster development of the productive forces than capitalism, but also because only socialism can eliminate the greed, corruption and injustice which are inherent in capitalism and other systems of exploitation. In recent years production has gone up, but the pernicious influence of capitalism and feudalism has not been reduced to a minimum. Instead, some evil things that had long been extinct after liberation have come to life again. We must be determined to change this situation as soon as possible, or how can the advantages of socialism be brought into full play? How can we effectively educate our people, especially the future generations? Material progress will suffer delays and setbacks unless we promote cultural and ideological progress as well. We can never succeed in revolution and construction if we rely on material conditions alone. In the past, no matter how small and weak our Party was, and no matter what difficulties it faced, we always maintained great combat-effectiveness thanks to our faith in Marxism and communism. Because we shared common ideals, we had strict discipline. Now, as in the past and in the future, that is our real strength. Today, some comrades no longer have a clear understanding of this truth. So it is hard for them to pay close attention to building a society that is advanced culturally and ideologically.

To build such a society we must first concentrate on bringing about a fundamental improvement in Party conduct and in general social conduct.

Improving Party conduct is the key to improving general social conduct. In consolidating the Party we must carry out the decision of the Second Plenary Session of the Twelfth Central Committee and succeed in all four tasks: achieving unity in thinking, improving conduct, strengthening discipline and purifying the Party organization. The Party Constitution contains clear provisions in this regard. Every Party organization must ask its members to measure themselves against each of the articles in the Constitution and to conduct self-criticism and criticism among themselves, and every Party organization must take disciplinary action when necessary. If all Party members set good examples, things will become easier.

The improvement of general social conduct must be accomplished through education, and education must conform to realities. To overcome major ideological weaknesses that are found among some cadres and other people and that affect social conduct, we must carry out in-depth investigations and assign proper people to conduct painstaking and convincing education. Over-simplified, one-sided or arbitrary arguments will not serve the purpose. Also, leading comrades at various levels must constantly explain the practical problems that affect people's everyday lives and the policy issues in which the masses show an interest. They should give facts and tell the people how things stand and what efforts the Party and government have made to solve the problems. In addition, they must act promptly to remedy situations about which the people justly complain. Only when the masses see concrete evidence that the Party and socialism are good will our teachings about ideals, discipline, communist ideology and patriotism be effective.

We must strengthen ideological and political work, reinforce the ranks of cadres in this field and do nothing to weaken them. At the same time, we should continue to guard against and crack down on serious crime and to prohibit all decadent practices that undermine standards of social conduct. In their economic activities and administrative and judicial work, enterprises and institutions must above all seek people's trust. They absolutely must not harm the people or extort money from them.

Ideological, cultural, educational and public health departments should make social benefit the sole criterion for their activities, and so should the enterprises affiliated with them. People engaged in ideological and cultural work should create more fine intellectual products, and the production, importation and circulation of undesirable ones should be resolutely banned. We must firmly oppose propaganda in favour of bourgeois liberalization, that is, in favour of the capitalist road. It goes without saying, however, that we should follow the policy of "letting a hundred flowers blossom, a hundred schools of thought contend" and uphold the freedoms guaranteed by the Constitution and laws of the state. With regard to erroneous ideological tendencies, we should follow the policy of persuasion and education and refrain from political movements and "mass criticism". Disciplinary action must be taken against those Party members who refuse to correct their errors, but under no circumstances should we repeat the "Left" mistake of resorting to summary measures and subjecting too many people to criticism.

If we accomplish all these tasks, we shall bring about a fundamental improvement in standards of social conduct.

Fourth, about the succession of new cadres to old and about theoretical study.

The succession of new cadres to old and co-operation between them have been going on fairly well over the past few years. A number of outstanding persons who are in the prime of life and have both ability and political integrity have been promoted to leading posts in both central and local departments of the Party, government and army. A satisfactory job has been done of replacing old members with new ones in the three central leading organs. As a result, the average age of Central Committee members, in particular, has been significantly reduced. A number of veteran cadres have taken the lead in abolishing the system of life tenure in leading posts, furthering the reform of the cadre system. This deserves special mention in the annals of our Party.

The members newly elected to the Central Committee and the ministers and provincial Party committee secretaries who have been appointed recently are comparatively young. They are generally in their fifties, with some just over forty. In the early days of the People's Republic, many of the ministers and provincial Party committee secretaries were of that age. What is most important for the young and middle-aged cadres when they take over from the old is to emulate their heroic spirit of revolutionary struggle. It is my hope that through your efforts the Party's fine traditions and work style will be carried forward. I once said that youth and professional competence alone are not enough. To this must be added a fine work style. I hope you will serve the people wholeheartedly, go among the masses and listen to their opinions, dare to speak the truth and oppose falsehood, not seek undeserved credit but perform real services, make a clear distinction between public and private interests, refrain from seeking personal favour at the expense of principle and appoint people on their merits rather than by favouritism.

We often say that the succession of new cadres to old provides the organizational guarantee for the continuity of our Party's policies. What does this continuity actually mean? It means, of course, the continuity of the domestic and foreign policies of independence, democracy, legality, opening to the outside world and invigorating the domestic economy, policies which we will by no means change. And all these policies are based on the Four Cardinal Principles. There is even less possibility of our changing or deviating from those principles. If we did, our society would be plunged into chaos. Stability and unity would be out of the question, and the construction, reform and rejuvenation of China would become no more than empty words.

Now I should like to propose a new requirement, not only for new cadres but for old ones as well: the study of Marxist theory. Some comrades may say: "We are busy now with construction, and what we need most is professional knowledge and managerial skills. What's the immediate use of studying Marxist theory?" Comrades, this is a misconception. Marxist theory is not a dogma but a guide to action. It calls on people to proceed from its basic principles and methodology and apply them to changing conditions so as to devise solutions to new problems. By this process, Marxist theory itself is further developed. Didn't the Russians succeed in their October Revolution and we in our revolution precisely because we both applied Marxist methods and principles? Times have changed and our tasks have changed. We are now building socialism with Chinese characteristics. There is indeed much new knowledge we need to master, but that makes it all the more necessary for us to study basic Marxist theory in light of the new situation. Because that is the only way we can become better able to apply the basic principles and methods of Marxism to the solution of the fundamental questions arising in the political, economic, social and cultural fields. And that is the only way we can both advance our cause and the theory of Marxism and also prevent comrades, particularly the newly promoted young and middle-aged comrades, from losing their bearings in the complex struggle. Therefore, I hope that the Central Committee will formulate a workable decision that will enable Party cadres at all levels, but especially leading cadres, to have some time in their busy schedules for study. That will enable them to become well versed in basic Marxist theory, and thus they will adhere more strictly to principles and work more systematically and with greater foresight and creativity. Only thus can our Party keep to the socialist road and go on building socialism with Chinese characteristics until we reach our ultimate goal —communism.

TALK AT A MEETING OF THE STANDING COMMITTEE OF THE POLITICAL BUREAU OF THE CENTRAL COMMITTEE

January 17, 1986

At the Party's Twelfth National Congress, held in September 1982, we said that we should promote socialist cultural and ideological progress so as to bring about within five years a fundamental improvement in conduct, both in the Party and in society at large. Since then three years and four months have elapsed and we have only one year and eight months left, so I'm afraid we may not be able to complete the task as scheduled. Nevertheless, we must redouble our efforts in this connection and not relax them for a single day.

To promote cultural and ideological progress and to raise standards of conduct both inside and outside the Party, we should start by dealing with specific cases of wrongdoing. We should move promptly to handle the cases of economic criminals, of people who in their dealings abroad have forfeited national and personal dignity and of persons who have served as enemy agents. The great majority of high-ranking cadres and their children are good. However, some of the children have divulged economic information, become involved in intelligence networks or sold information and documents. We should concentrate on investigating typical cases of law-breaking by the children of senior cadres, senior cadres themselves and well-known public figures, because crimes committed by these people cause the most serious damage. When these cases are discovered and dealt with, they will have the most effect and will show our determination to surmount all obstacles to promote cultural and ideological progress. It doesn't matter much if some small fry slip through the net; of course, I don't mean that we can lie back and take it easy on that account. But if we do a thorough job with these cases, we shall have an excellent chance of success; otherwise, it's hopeless. High-ranking cadres whose family members have been involved in criminal activities should take a firm, clear-cut attitude towards those activities and resolutely support the judicial organs that are in charge of their cases. Anyone who has engaged in criminal activities must be dealt with in accordance with Party discipline and state law. Vigorous action must be taken, and we can't be too tender-hearted. Take the case of Yang Xiaomin in Qinghai Province for example. For years a series of provincial Party secretaries took no action on it. Now it has been dealt with at last, and that is good. Dealing with that kind of case can have a great impact on the society.

The death penalty cannot be abolished, and some criminals must be sentenced to death. Recently I have read some relevant documents, from which I understand there are a great many habitual criminals who, on being released after a few years' remoulding through forced labour, resume their criminal activities, each time becoming more skilful and more experienced in coping with the public security and judicial organs. Why don't we have some of them executed according to law? Why don't we punish severely, according to law, some of those people who traffic in women and children, who make a living by playing on people's superstitions or who organize reactionary secret societies, and some of those habitual criminals who refuse to reform despite repeated attempts to educate them. Some of them must be executed, but of course we have to be very careful in such matters. [*At this point Comrade Chen Yun remarked that executing some of them could help save a large number of cadres.*] Those who have merely made mistakes in the political and ideological sphere but have not violated state law should not be given any criminal sanctions, let alone the death penalty. But some of the perpetrators of serious economic or other crimes must be executed as required by law. Generally speaking, the problem now is that we are too soft on criminals. As a matter of fact, execution is one of the indispensable means of education. [*Comrade Chen Yun again intervened here to say that executing one could serve as a warning to a hundred.*] Nowadays the death penalty is generally reserved for murderers only, but how about those who have committed other serious crimes? In Guangdong Province prostitution is rampant—why don't we crack down on the worst proprietors of brothels? The ones who refuse to reform after being jailed and released several times should be severely punished as required by law. Some government functionaries have committed economic crimes so serious that they have caused the state financial losses amounting to as much as several million, or even ten million, yuan. Why can't they be sentenced to death in accordance with the Criminal Law? For example, in 1952 two persons were executed, one by the name of Liu Qingshan and another by the name of Zhang Zishan,[20] and that had a great impact on the society as a whole. Things are different now, and the effect would not be so great. To show our determination, we would have to execute several more than two.

The Secretariat has done an excellent job of improving Party conduct and general social conduct. I suggest that if it spends two more years on this work, it will achieve noticeable results. Success in this area will advance reform and construction. With all the resolve in the world, it will still take at least ten years' worth of effort to restore Party and social conduct to the standards of the best period of the 1950s. The political line and the various policies set forth by the Central Committee are correct, and we must continue to carry out the reform and to open to the outside world. But there are many failings in our management and other work, and some Party cadres' style of work and behaviour are shockingly bad. So in the movement to improve Party conduct, we should check up on Party members and expel some of them. Improvement in this area will demand at least ten years' painstaking work, for it takes that long to educate people. The ten-year "cultural revolution" had a pernicious influence on the younger generation, and it is precisely owing to that influence that a small number of students have recently stirred up trouble. In the effort to rectify Party conduct and raise general social standards in the past two years people have often been irresolute in many ways. For example, even when handling a very clear case, they have found it necessary to run around investigating, getting approval from this one and that, and then repeating the whole process, with the result that for years the case was never settled. As soon as we have ascertained the facts and got to the bottom of a case, we should pass judgement on it. Here too we need resolute and prompt action.

We should redouble our efforts beginning with the current Meeting of Cadres of the Central Organs. The meeting has been going on for less than ten days, but it has already received warm response from all quarters. The speeches delivered at that meeting by several comrades should be published as the Central Committee's Document No. 1 for 1986.

Our original idea was right: in our efforts to realize the modernization programme we must attend to two things and not just one. By this I mean that we must promote economic development and at the same time build a legal system. The Party has its discipline and the state has its law. Why is the principle of upholding the people's democratic dictatorship included in the Four Cardinal Principles? It is because if we practise democracy within the ranks of the people without exercising dictatorship over the saboteurs, we cannot maintain political stability and unity or succeed in the modernization drive.

Starting from this year, we shall work really hard for two more years. We have been fairly successful in economic development, and the economic situation is gratifying. This is quite an achievement for our country. But if standards of social conduct are deteriorating, what's the use of achieving economic development? Worse, deteriorating social standards will in turn lead to a qualitative change in the economy, eventually producing a society in which embezzlement, theft and bribery run rampant. That's why we cannot do without the Four Cardinal Principles, without dictatorship over the saboteurs. This dictatorship can ensure the smooth progress of the drive for socialist modernization and deal effectively with persons whose actions undermine our construction work.

I agree with the way the Secretariat has been doing this work.

REMARKS ON THE DOMESTIC ECONOMIC SITUATION*

June 10, 1986

In general, the present economic situation is good. But how about the future? What problems or obstacles are we going to run into? As I see it, there are two or three problems that might hold up the growth of our economy.

The first is agriculture, which is essentially a problem of grain. If we have a setback in agriculture, it will be impossible for us to recover in just three to five years. Let's make a rough calculation: if in the year 2000 there are 1.2 billion people and each person consumes 400 kilogrammes of grain, we shall have to produce 480 million tons that year. To reach this goal, we shall have to increase output by more than 5 million tons annually from now on. But right now grain production is increasing slowly, and there are already some places where people are not able to raise pigs because there is not enough grain for feed. An expert has predicted that if there is only a modest investment in rural capital construction and productivity remains low, China's agriculture will enter a new period of stagnation. This is something we have to watch out for. In managing the economy as a whole, we should give agriculture an appropriate priority, always bearing in mind our general goal of producing 480 million tons of grain in the year 2000. We should try to avoid having once

* Remarks to leading members of the Central Committee of the Chinese Communist Party who had made a report on the current economic situation.

again to import large amounts of grain a few years from now, because that will retard the growth of our economy.

The second problem is foreign exchange. Will the growth of the economy be impeded by a shortage of foreign exchange and a deficit in foreign trade? We must try to reduce that deficit year by year. If we don't, we shall be held back, and sustained, steady economic development will be out of the question. Some Japanese visitors said recently that there were many things that China could export, many things that could be sold on the Japanese market. They said that we didn't know enough about world markets. We could expand the Hongkong market by supplying it with larger quantities of fruit and vegetables. We could set up special bases to produce fresh produce, livestock, poultry, fish and so forth for export. At first glance, it seems that exports like these could not bring in much foreign exchange. But when all the small earnings were accumulated they would add up to a large amount. We should find out what we can send to the Southeast Asian market. And we should think about ways to increase the export of coal. We should also consider how to raise the quality of products. I said last year that we should not just emphasize quantity; we should put quality above everything else. The key to ensuring good sales of our exports is to improve their quality. Without high quality, they cannot be competitive on the world market. Under the planning method we copied from the Soviet Union, we used to calculate only output value, concentrating on quantity to the neglect of quality. As a matter of fact, it is the quality of products that matters the most. In short, it is of strategic importance to reduce the deficit in foreign trade year by year. If we don't do that, our economy will eventually go into decline.

The third problem is political restructuring. As it stands,

our political structure is not adapted to the current situation. Political restructuring should be included in the reform—indeed, it should be regarded as the hallmark of the reform as a whole. We must streamline the administration, delegate real powers to lower levels and broaden the scope of socialist democracy, so as to bring into play the initiative of the masses and the grass-roots organizations. At present, the number of organizations, instead of being reduced, has actually increased. What happens is this: here, we are calling for the delegation of powers to lower levels, but out there people at higher levels are taking those powers back by establishing companies that are actually government organs. The more organs you have, the more staff members there are, and they all have to find something to do. They keep a tight grip on power, making it impossible for the lower levels to act on their own. We have to make a careful analysis to find out how to go about political reform. Early in 1980 it was suggested that we reform the political structure, but no concrete measures to do so were worked out. Now it is time for us to place political reform on the agenda. Otherwise, organizational overlapping, overstaffing, bureacratism, sluggishness, unreliability and the taking back of powers granted to lower levels will weigh us down and retard the progress of our economic reform.

I think the reform is proceeding smoothly in general. Through the reform we shall create the necessary conditions for sustained, steady economic growth. We are now advancing with heavy loads on our backs. One such load, which is getting heavier all the time, is the tens of billions of yuan's worth of price subsidies provided annually by the state. Sooner or later we must find a systematic, appropriate solution to this problem. Unless enterprises are given authority, they will have no power to make decisions and hence have no obligations to fulfil; it is the upper levels that will be held responsible for their success or failure. Under such circumstances, how can our work be done well? And how can the initiative of the masses be brought into play? So the current reform must be carried on.

REFORM THE POLITICAL STRUCTURE AND STRENGTHEN THE PEOPLE'S SENSE OF LEGALITY*

June 28, 1986

Some comrades have raised the question of who should be in charge of rectifying Party conduct and who should be in charge of correcting unhealthy tendencies in society at large. As a matter of fact, this is not the key question. The key question is the relationship between the Party and the government. It is not appropriate for the Party to concern itself with matters that fall within the scope of the law. If the Party intervenes in everything, the people will never acquire a sense of the rule of law. The Party should concern itself with inner-Party discipline, leaving problems that fall within the scope of the law to the state and the government. So the crux of the matter is the relationship between the Party and government, a question of the political structure of our country. I suggest that we give it further consideration and I think we can straighten it out at the Party's Thirteenth National Congress, to be held next year. Once this question is settled, the question of who should take charge of rectifying Party conduct and who should take charge of correcting unhealthy tendencies in society at large will be decided accordingly. Right now we are focusing on rectifying Party

* Talk at the Standing Committee of the Political Bureau of the Central Committee.

conduct, but at the same time in the society as a whole we are trying to strengthen the legal system. Our country has no tradition of observing and enforcing laws. Since the Third Plenary Session of the Eleventh Central Committee we have been working on establishing a legal system—that is indispensable. People's sense of legality is related to their educational level. One reason for the high crime rate among young people is that their level of education is too low. To strengthen legality, therefore, the most important thing is to educate people, especially about the law. This education should begin at an early age and be carried out in all our primary and middle schools. There are young people today who are simply lawless and have no scruples about committing crimes. In short, letting the Party take charge of matters that come within the scope of the law and including criminal activities in the category of Party conduct, as something to be dealt with by the Central Commission for Discipline Inspection, will not help cultivate the sense of legality among all our people. In cracking down on crime and correcting unhealthy tendencies, we should use the legal system in criminal cases and education in non-criminal ones. We should sum up our experience in this respect so as to improve our work.

In addition, we should sum up our experience of the way in which the Party exercises leadership over the government. Beginning from the Third Plenary Session of the Eleventh Central Committee, we have been calling for a distinction to be made between the responsibilities of the Party and those of the government. We uphold the Party's leadership, but the problem is whether the Party is doing a good job of leading. It should give effective leadership and not intervene in too many matters. The Central Committee should take the lead in this regard. What I am proposing will not weaken the Party's leadership. On the contrary, its leadership will be weakened if it tries to take responsibility for too many areas. I'm afraid that's how we have to look at it. The last time I talked with some comrades about economic work I called their attention to the necessity of reforming the political structure, including the need to solve this problem of Party interference. Of course, there are other problems that have to be solved in a reform of the political structure, such as the overstaffing of administrative organs and the sluggish pace of work. The large numbers of staff have to find something to do, so many institutions, by establishing companies, have simply taken back the powers that had been delegated to the lower levels. While we are demanding that powers be transferred to lower levels, they are taking them back. I am told that some comrades think there were also man-made causes for the lower economic growth rate in the first half of this year, and that this tendency of higher levels to take powers back was one of them. Our policy is to continue the devolution of powers, but many institutions are resisting it. As a result, the enterprises are deprived of their powers and their initiative withers. So this is one of the reasons why the growth rate has gone down. I suggest that all our comrades, especially those in the Secretariat, consider this question of reforming the political structure. We shouldn't take any action until we have drawn up a workable plan. We can first spend a year or so making investigations and identifying the problems. In the final analysis, all our other reforms depend on the success of the political reform, because it is human beings who will—or will not—carry them out. For instance, we encourage devolution of powers, but other people take powers back. What can we do about it? There are other problems too. The reform of the political structure and the reform of the economic structure are interdependent and should be co-ordinated. Without political reform, economic reform cannot succeed, because the first obstacle to be overcome is people's resistance.

In the first half of this year we have scored some achievements in rectifying Party conduct. But let's not overestimate them, for they are only a beginning. When we said that we needed to spend two years concentrating on this work, we didn't mean that that would be the end of it. Of course, we don't necessarily need to set up a special organ for this purpose, but the work will have to continue throughout the period of the reform. Our efforts to open to the outside world and invigorate the domestic economy are bound to have some undesirable side effects. If we fail to cope with them, our work will take the wrong direction. So this is going to be a long-term task. As long as we pursue the policies of opening to the outside world and invigorating the domestic economy, we shall have to continue our efforts to improve Party conduct, to correct bad tendencies in the society at large and to crack down on crime. That is the only way to ensure correct implementation of those policies.

TO ENSURE DEVELOPMENT OF THE PRODUCTIVE FORCES WE MUST REFORM THE POLITICAL STRUCTURE*

September 3, 1986

Our reform of the economic structure is going smoothly on the whole. Nevertheless, as it proceeds we shall inevitably encounter obstacles. It is true that there are people, both inside and outside our Party, who are not in favour of the reform, but there are not many who strongly oppose it. The important thing is that our political structure does not meet the needs of the economic reform. So unless we modify our political structure, we shall be unable to advance the economic reform or even to preserve the gains we have made so far.

When we first raised the question of reform we had in mind, among other things, reform of the political structure. Whenever we move a step forward in economic reform, we are made keenly aware of the need to change the political structure. If we fail to do that, it will stunt the growth of the productive forces and impede our drive for modernization. The content of the political reform is still under discussion, because this question is very complex. Since every reform measure will involve a wide range of people, have profound

* Excerpt from a talk with Takeiri Yoshikatsu, Chairman of the Central Executive Committee of the Komei Party of Japan.

repercussions in many areas and affect the interests of countless individuals, we shall inevitably run into obstacles, and it is therefore especially important for us to proceed with caution. First of all we have to determine the scope of the political restructuring and decide where to begin. We shall start with one or two reforms and not try to do everything all at once, because we don't want to make a mess of things. It is such a difficult and complex task that we have not yet made up our minds how to begin.

In essence, the purpose of political restructuring is to overcome bureaucratism and stimulate the initiative of the people and of the grass-roots units. Through the reform, we intend to solve the problem of the rule of law in China as opposed to the rule of man and to straighten out the relationship between the Party and the government. We should be firm about leadership by the Party, but the question of how the Party should exercise its leadership must be put on the agenda. The Party should lead well, but its responsibilities must be separated from those of the government. Over the past few years we have successfully experimented in a number of factories with the system under which the director assumes full responsibility. We have also done a great deal of work to delegate powers to lower levels, but without much success. For one thing, while we are delegating powers to the lower levels, other people are taking them back by establishing more organs, so the grass-roots units can't function independently. Besides, we have to streamline the administrative structure. At present, leading organs at various levels have so many people on the staff that work has to be found to keep them busy. This creates many problems, the worst of which are that the flow of business is sluggish, decision-making is slow and problems are dealt with inefficiently. All this has chilled the enthusiasm of people in the grass-roots units. And there are other problems that we have not yet solved satisfactorily, such as how to find and make use of skilled people and how to develop socialist democracy. We have to encourage democracy so as to stimulate the initiative of the people and of the grass-roots units.

At the Sixth Plenary Session of the Party's Twelfth National Congress, which is to be held shortly, we won't have time to work out any decisions on the reform of the political structure. Still, we shall deal with certain aspects of it. We shall also determine which aspect to begin with. In a country as vast and complex as ours, reform is no easy task. So we must be very cautious about setting policies and make no decision until we are quite sure it is the right one.

WE MUST HAVE A PLAN FOR THE REFORM OF THE POLITICAL STRUCTURE*

September 13, 1986

If we do not institute a reform of our political structure, it will be difficult to carry out the reform of our economic structure. Separation of the responsibilities of the Party and the government comes under the heading of political reform, and that raises the question of how a Party committee should exercise leadership. The answer is that it should deal only with major issues and not with minor ones. Organizational overlapping is one of the biggest obstacles to reform. Local Party committees should not establish departments to take charge of economic affairs; those affairs should be the responsibility of local governments. However, that's not the way it is at present.

We have to discuss what the content of political reform should be. Since, in my opinion, its purposes are to bring the initiative of the masses into play, to increase efficiency and to overcome bureaucratism, its content should be as follows. First we should separate the Party and the government and decide how the Party can exercise leadership most effectively. This is the key. Second, we should transfer some of the powers of the central authorities to local authorities in order to straighten out relations between the two. At the same time, local authorities should likewise transfer some of their pow-

* Excerpt from remarks made after hearing a report from the Finance and Economics Leadership Group of the Central Committee.

ers to lower levels. Third, we should streamline the administrative structure, and this is related to the devolution of powers. One further task will be to raise efficiency. The content of political reform has to be clarified and details worked out. We must set a starting date—one that is not too remote. At the National Party Congress next year we shall draw up a plan, in which I think the separation of the Party and the government should be given first priority. However, in reforming our political structure we must not imitate the West, and no liberalization should be allowed. Of course our present structure of leadership has some advantages. For example, it enables us to make quick decisions, while if we place too much emphasis on a need for checks and balances, problems may arise.

REMARKS AT THE SIXTH PLENARY SESSION OF THE PARTY'S TWELFTH CENTRAL COMMITTEE*

September 28, 1986

With regard to the question of opposing bourgeois liberalization, I am the one who has talked about it most often and most insistently. Why? First, because there is now a trend of thought—that is, liberalization—among the masses, especially among the young people. Second, because this trend has found support from the sidelines. For example, there have been some comments from people in Hongkong and Taiwan who are all opposed to our Four Cardinal Principles and who think we should introduce the capitalist system lock, stock and barrel, as if that were the only genuine modernization. What in fact is this liberalization? It is an attempt to turn China's present policies in the direction of capitalism. The exponents of this trend are trying to lead us towards capitalism. That is why I have explained time and again that our modernization programme is a socialist one. Our decision to apply the open policy and assimilate useful things from capitalist societies was made only to supplement the development of our socialist productive forces.

---

* Remarks during discussion of the Draft Resolution of the Central Committee on the Guiding Principles for Building a Socialist Society with an Advanced Culture and Ideology.

We all remember that in 1980, after the defeat of the Gang of Four, the National People's Congress adopted a resolution to delete from the Constitution the provision concerning the right of citizens to "speak out freely, air their views fully, hold great debates and put up big-character posters". Why did we do this? Because there was an ideological trend of liberalization. If that trend had been allowed to spread, it would have undermined our political stability and unity, without which construction would be out of the question.

Liberalization itself is bourgeois in nature—there is no such thing as proletarian or socialist liberalization. Liberalization by itself means antagonism to our current policies and systems and a wish to revise them. In fact, exponents of liberalization want to lead us down the road to capitalism. That's why we call it bourgeois liberalization. It doesn't matter if the term has been used elsewhere in other contexts, for our current politics demands that we use it in the resolution, and I am in favour of it.

It seems to me that the struggle against liberalization will have to be carried on not only now but for the next 10 or 20 years. If we fail to check this trend, it will merge with undesirable foreign things that will inevitably find their way into China because of our open policy and become a battering ram used against our modernization programme. This is something we cannot afford to ignore. If you have read some of the comments that have been made by people in Hongkong and by bourgeois scholars in foreign countries, you will see that most of them insist that we should liberalize, or say that there are no human rights in China. These commentators oppose the very things we believe in and hope that we will change. But we shall continue to raise problems and solve them in the light of the realities in China.

REFORM THE POLITICAL STRUCTURE IN THE LIGHT OF DOMESTIC CONDITIONS*

September 29, 1986

Both of our countries are carrying out reforms. In the reform of political structure, many of the specific measures we take in China will probably be different from yours. This only goes to show that you make your decisions in light of the particular conditions in your own country while we make ours in light of our own conditions. Since conditions in China and Poland are different, the measures we take will be different too. Our general objectives, however, are the same. In essence, they consist of the following: (1) to consolidate the socialist system, (2) to develop the socialist productive forces, and (3) to expand socialist democracy in order to bring the initiative of the people into full play. The chief purpose of mobilizing the people's initiative is to develop the productive forces and raise living standards, thus increasing the strength of our socialist country and consolidating and improving the socialist system. We can therefore understand the policies and measures you have adopted. Since both our countries are undertaking a great experiment, we cannot expect to accomplish the tasks we set ourselves all at once, and sometimes mistakes may be made. That doesn't matter.

---

* Excerpt from a talk with Wojciech Jaruzelski, First Secretary of the Central Committee of the Polish United Workers' Party and Chairman of the State Council of the People's Republic of Poland.

If we explore possibilities boldly but with great care and prudence, we can correct our mistakes in good time. Minor errors are in fact inevitable, but we should try to avoid major ones. As long as we proceed with caution, there is nothing to be afraid of. Both of our political structures were copied from the Soviet model. It seems to me that the Soviet Union's own political structure has not been very successful. But even if the Soviet Union had achieved one hundred per cent success, would its political structure be suited to realities in China? Would it be suited to realities in Poland? Conditions vary from one country to another.

SOME IDEAS ON THE REFORM OF THE POLITICAL STRUCTURE*

November 9, 1986

So far as the reform of our political structure is concerned, we haven't sorted things out yet. But lately I've been thinking it should have three objectives.

The first objective is to ensure the continuing vitality of the Party and the state. This means that our cadres must be young. A few years ago we set forth four requirements for cadres: that they should be more revolutionary, younger, better educated and more competent professionally. We have made some progress in this respect over the last few years, but that's just a beginning. This first objective is not something that can be achieved within three years or five. We shall be doing well if we achieve it in fifteen. By the time of the Party's Thirteenth National Congress next year, we shall have taken a first step towards our goal, but that's all. By the Fourteenth National Congress, we expect to have taken another step, and by the Fifteenth to have reached our objective. This is not something people of our age can accomplish, but it is vitally important for us to set the goal. It would be wonderful if someday China had a contingent of fine 30-to-40-year-old government officials, managers, scientists, writers and specialists in other fields. It is essential to introduce measures in various areas, including education, to encourage

---

* Excerpt from a talk with Prime Minister Yasuhiro Nakasone of Japan.

young people. Strictly speaking, we are only taking our first steps in this regard. There are many problems to be studied and many measures to be taken, but we must act on the matter.

The second objective of political structural reform is to eliminate bureaucratism and increase efficiency. One reason for low efficiency is that organizations are overstaffed and their work proceeds at a snail's pace. But the main reason is that we have not separated the responsibilities of the Party from those of the government, so that the Party often takes over the work of the government, and the two have many overlapping organs. We must uphold leadership by the Party, which is one of the characteristics of China, and never abandon it, but the Party should exercise its leadership effectively. It's several years already since we first raised this problem of efficiency, but we still have no clear idea as to how to solve it. Unless we increase efficiency, we shall not succeed in our drive for modernization. In the world today, mankind is progressing at a tremendous pace. Especially in science and technology, if we lag only one year behind, it will be very hard to catch up. So we have to increase our efficiency. Of course this is not just a question of separating the Party from the government; there are many other problems to be solved.

The third objective of political reform is to stimulate the initiative of grass-roots units and of workers, peasants and intellectuals. One thing we have learned from our experience in economic reform over the last few years is that the first step is to release the people's initiative by delegating powers to lower levels. That is what we did in the countryside. Factories, mines and other enterprises should do likewise in order to motivate workers and intellectuals, democratizing management by letting them participate in it. The same applies to every other field of endeavour.

Only with a vigorous leadership that has eliminated bureaucratism, raised efficiency and mobilized the grass-roots units and the rank and file can we have real hope of success in our modernization drive.

Right now we are studying the question of whether the political structural reform should focus on these three objectives, or whether there should be only two or perhaps four or five. It is less than a year until we convene the Party's Thirteenth National Congress, so we shall not be able to draw up comprehensive guidelines for the reform in time to present them there. We shall probably present a few at that Congress and then work out a few more in 1988 and 1989. At the moment all we are sure of is that the reform of our political structure is necessary and urgent. Since we've never had any experience in this area, we shall have to feel our way as we go along.

TAKE A CLEAR-CUT STAND AGAINST BOURGEOIS LIBERALIZATION*

December 30, 1986

The recent student unrest is not going to lead to any major disturbances. But because of its nature it must be taken very seriously. Firm measures must be taken against any student who creates trouble at Tiananmen Square. The rules and regulations on marches and demonstrations promulgated by the Standing Committee of the Municipal People's Congress of Beijing have the force of law and should be resolutely enforced. No concessions should be made in this matter. In the beginning, we mainly used persuasion, which is as it should be in dealing with student demonstrators. But if any of them disturb public order or violate the law, they must be dealt with unhesitatingly. Persuasion includes application of the law. When a disturbance breaks out in a place, it's because the leaders there didn't take a firm, clear-cut stand. This is not a problem that has arisen in just one or two places or in just the last couple of years; it is the result of failure over the past several years to take a firm, clear-cut stand against bourgeois liberalization. It is essential to adhere firmly to the Four Cardinal Principles; otherwise bourgeois liberalization will spread unchecked—and that has been the root cause of the problem. But this student unrest is also a good thing, insofar as it is a reminder to us.

---

* Remarks on recent student disturbances, made to some leading members of the Central Committee of the Chinese Communist Party.

I have read Fang Lizhi's speeches.[21] He doesn't sound like a Communist Party member at all. Why do we keep people like him in the Party? He should be expelled, not just persuaded to quit. There are some people who still hold to their opinions but who say they will not get involved in student disturbances. That's fine. You can reserve your opinions, so long as you don't take part in activities against the Party or socialism. Wang Ruowang in Shanghai is very presumptuous.[22] He should have been expelled from the Party long ago—why this delay? A rumour is going around Shanghai to the effect that there is disagreement in the Central Committee as to whether we should uphold the Four Cardinal Principles and oppose liberalization, and that there is therefore a layer of protection. That's why people in Shanghai are taking a wait-and-see attitude towards the disturbances. We have to admit that on the ideological and theoretical front both central and local authorities have been weak and have lost ground. They have taken a laissez-faire attitude towards bourgeois liberalization, so that good people find no support while bad people go wild. Good people don't dare to speak out, as if they were in the wrong. But they are not in the wrong at all. We must stand up for the Four Cardinal Principles and especially the people's democratic dictatorship. There is no way to ensure continued political stability and unity without the people's democratic dictatorship. People who confuse right and wrong, who turn black into white, who start rumours and spread slanders can't be allowed to go around with impunity stirring the masses up to make trouble. A few years ago we punished according to law some exponents of liberalization who broke the law. Did that bring discredit on us? No, China's image was not damaged. On the contrary, the prestige of our country is steadily growing.

In developing our democracy, we cannot simply copy bourgeois democracy, or introduce the system of a balance of three powers. I have often criticized people in power in the United States, saying that actually they have three governments. Of course, the American bourgeoisie uses this system in dealing with other countries, but when it comes to internal affairs, the three branches often pull in different directions, and that makes trouble. We cannot adopt such a system.

In carrying out the open policy, learning foreign technologies and utilizing foreign capital, we mean to promote socialist construction, not to deviate from the socialist road. We intend to develop the productive forces, expand ownership by the entire people and raise the people's income. The purpose of allowing some regions and some people to become prosperous before others is to enable all of them to prosper eventually. We have to make sure that there is no polarization of society—that's what socialism means. We work for common prosperity, but we permit certain disparities of income.

Without leadership by the Communist Party and without socialism, there is no future for China. This truth has been demonstrated in the past, and it will be demonstrated again in future. When we succeed in raising China's per capita GNP to $4,000 and everyone is prosperous, that will better demonstrate the superiority of socialism over capitalism, it will point the way for three quarters of the world's population and it will provide further proof of the correctness of Marxism. Therefore, we must confidently keep to the socialist road and uphold the Four Cardinal Principles.

We cannot do without dictatorship. We must not only affirm the need for it but exercise it when necessary. Of course, we must be cautious about resorting to dictatorial means and make as few arrests as possible. But if some people attempt to provoke bloodshed, what are we going to do about it? We should first expose their plot and then do our best to avoid shedding blood, even if that means some of our own people get hurt. However, ringleaders who have violated the law must be sentenced according to law. Unless we are prepared to do that, it will be impossible to put an end to disturbances. If we take no action and back down, we shall only have more trouble down the road.

In the recent student unrest, the democratic parties have taken a correct position, and so have well-known democrats such as Zhou Gucheng,[23] Fei Xiaotong[24] and Qian Weichang.[25] Unfortunately, we cannot say the same of some of our own Party members.

This time, we have to take action against those who openly oppose socialism and the Communist Party. This may make some waves, but that's nothing to be afraid of. We must resolutely impose sanctions on Fang Lizhi, Liu Binyan[26] and Wang Ruowang, who are so arrogant that they want to remould the Communist Party. What qualifications do they have to be Party members?

Originally, I had not intended to say anything at the Sixth Plenary Session of the Twelfth Central Committee. But later, I felt I had to intervene to ask that there be included in the resolution a few words on the necessity of combating bourgeois liberalization. Apparently, my remarks on that occasion had no great effect. I understand they were never disseminated throughout the Party.

I still haven't changed my mind about opposing spiritual pollution. I have agreed to have the full text of my speech at the Second Plenary Session of the Twelfth Central Committee included in a new collection of my works [see pp.24-40 above].

The struggle against bourgeois liberalization will last for

at least 20 years. Democracy can develop only gradually, and we cannot copy Western systems. If we did, that would only make a mess of everything. Our socialist construction can only be carried out under leadership, in an orderly way and in an environment of stability and unity. That's why I lay such emphasis on the need for high ideals and strict discipline. Bourgeois liberalization would plunge the country into turmoil once more. Bourgeois liberalization means rejection of the Party's leadership; there would be nothing to unite our one billion people, and the Party itself would lose all power to fight. A party like that would be no better than a mass organization; how could it be expected to lead the people in construction?

The struggle against the bourgeois Rightists in 1957 was carried somewhat too far, and the mistakes made should be corrected. But that doesn't mean that we have negated this struggle as a whole.

The struggle against bourgeois liberalization is also indispensable. We should not be afraid that it will damage our reputation abroad. China must take its own road and build socialism with Chinese characteristics—that is the only way China can have a future. We must show foreigners that China's political situation is stable. If our country were plunged into disorder and our nation reduced to a heap of loose sand, how could we ever prosper? The reason the imperialists were able to bully us in the past was precisely that we were a heap of loose sand.

Dealing with the student disturbances is a serious matter. Leading cadres should take a clear-cut stand; that will help the masses to see things more clearly. The three articles relating to the disturbances that were published in *Renmin Ribao* (*People's Daily*) were well written, and so was the editorial that appeared in *Beijing Ribao* (*Beijing Daily*) entitled "Big-Character Posters Are Not Protected by the Law". The remarks made by Li Ruihuan[27] were also good. The fact that the leading cadres take an unequivocal stand encourages those who are firmly opposed to disturbances and helps to persuade those who are undecided on the matter. Disturbance can be checked if the leaders take a strong stand.

CLEAR AWAY OBSTACLES AND ADHERE TO THE POLICIES OF REFORM AND OF OPENING TO THE OUTSIDE WORLD*

January 13, 1987

Recently some of our students created disturbances. These disturbances were different in nature from those of September 18, 1985, when students took to the streets. We are now handling this matter. Actually, what concerns us is not the small number of college and university students, the one or two per cent of the total in the country, who took part. That is not really the problem—a few students who take to the streets cannot affect the overall situation. The problem is that there has been some confusion in our ideological work and students have not been given strong, effective guidance. That is a major mistake. We must change this situation and tell our young people about our past. At the same time we should expose those persons who have acted out of ulterior motives, because this time they have adopted slogans that clearly express opposition to Communist Party leadership and the socialist road. Certain individuals have made exceedingly pernicious statements, trying to incite people to action. They oppose Communist Party leadership and the socialist system, they call for total westernization of China and adop-

---

* Excerpt from a talk with Noboru Takeshita, Secretary-General of the Liberal Democratic Party of Japan.

tion of the whole capitalist system of the West. These instigators are well-known persons, and we have to do something about them. They are to be found, of all places, inside the Communist Party. The Communist Party has its discipline. Actually every party in the world has its own discipline. This time we are going to make a point of checking up on discipline.

A little trouble stirred up by students won't have any great impact, much less bring us down, especially when the trouble-makers amount to just one or two per cent of all college and university students. In short, there is one point I'd like to assure our friends of, and that is, we shall handle problems like this in an appropriate way. Even if these disturbances had been much more widespread, they would have had no effect on the foundations of our state or on the policies we have established. When we have dealt with those problems, our political stability and unity will only be enhanced and our established principles and policies—including the policies of opening to the outside world, reform and construction—will only be carried out more smoothly, steadily and perseveringly. In settling this matter, we shall of course sum up our experience and gradually overcome our weaknesses—bureaucratism, for example. In this way we shall eventually turn something negative into something positive and help to clarify the thinking of both the leaders and the people.

It is no simple thing to introduce reform and modernize our country. But we have never harboured any illusions that it would all be easy. There will inevitably be interference from various directions, including both the Right and the "Left". If in the past we have paid too much attention to interference from the "Left" to the neglect of that from the Right, the recent student unrest has reminded us that we should be more on guard against the latter. In this sense, the recent events will turn out to have had a positive effect. I am convinced that our future accomplishments will be a further demonstration of the correctness of our present line, principles and policies. Problems will be solved naturally, so long as we go on developing in the way we have during the past eight years, try to overcome interference from any side, and continue to grow and advance steadily and to raise the people's standard of living. In short, we have to clear away the obstacles. Without political stability and unity, it would be impossible for us to go on with construction, let alone to pursue the open policy. Opening to the outside world is no simple matter, and reform is even more difficult. None of these endeavours can succeed in the absence of stability and unity. Furthermore, the reform must be conducted in an orderly way. That is to say, we must be at once daring and cautious, and review our experience frequently so as to advance more surely. Without order, we shall have to devote all our energies to combating interference of one kind or another, and that would be the end of the reform.

We should explain to the students who have been involved in disturbances what is at stake. A few mild remonstrations won't serve the purpose. It is essential to explain clearly to them what is right and what is wrong, what is beneficial and what is harmful. By what is right and what is wrong I mean what serves the fundamental interests of the country and what damages them. And by what is beneficial and what is harmful I mean what helps us to achieve the basic socialist objectives we have set for this century and the next and what hinders us from doing so. This is the way to show our concern for the young people and to give them genuine guidance. Since the Third Plenary Session of the Eleventh Central Committee, held in December 1978, we have been opposing anarchism and ultra-individualism. But today some people are vainly trying to make our society absolutely lawless. How can we allow that to happen? Even capitalist society doesn't allow people to defy the law, and far less can we, who uphold the socialist system and want to build socialism with Chinese characteristics. You are very concerned about this question in China. I should like to assure our friends that the student unrest will not lead to major trouble. It will have no effect on our established principles and policies; it will have no effect on our reforms or our opening to the outside world. It has reminded not only ourselves but our friends as well that to understand China's problems, one must recognize their complexity. China is a country which has more than one billion people and dozens of nationalities and which has traversed a tortuous road over the more than 30 years since the founding of the People's Republic. So it is not surprising that such disturbances should have occurred. We should try to prevent them from spreading, but even if ten times more people were involved, they would not affect the foundations of our state or make us alter our policies, because they are correct and the people have benefited from them. During the "cultural revolution" we had what was called mass democracy. In those days people thought that rousing the masses to headlong action was democracy and that it would solve all problems. But it turned out that when the masses were roused to headlong action, the result was civil war. We have learned our lesson from history.

PROMOTE EDUCATION IN THE FOUR CARDINAL PRINCIPLES AND ADHERE TO THE POLICIES OF REFORM AND OF OPENING TO THE OUTSIDE WORLD*

January 20, 1987

Recently two major events have taken place in our country: one was the student disturbances and the other the replacement of the General Secretary of our Party. Why did the students create disturbances? Basically, it was because of weak leadership. We call for upholding the Four Cardinal Principles, that is, for keeping to the socialist road, upholding the people's democratic dictatorship, upholding leadership by the Communist Party and upholding Marxism-Leninism and Mao Zedong Thought. We must conduct constant education in these principles among our people. In the past few years we have witnessed the emergence of bourgeois liberalization, an ideological trend that has not been effectively countered. Although I have warned against this trend on many occasions, our Party has failed to provide adequate leadership in combating it. This was a major mistake made by Comrade Hu Yaobang. So at an enlarged meeting, the Political Bureau of the Central Committee accepted his resignation from the post of General Secretary and elected Comrade Zhao Ziyang Acting General Secretary. The two events are related. They

---

* Excerpt from a talk with Prime Minister Robert Mugabe of Zimbabwe.

are by no means minor matters, but our Party has been quite capable of dealing with them. Comrade Hu Yaobang's case has been handled reasonably, or quite gently I should say, and it was settled very smoothly. The handling of these two events will affect neither our Party's line, principles and policies, nor our policy of opening up both domestically and internationally, nor the reform of our economic and political structures. It will only help to clarify the thinking of the Party and the people and strengthen our conviction that we are on the right road. In spite of these events, things will go on as usual and there will be no changes at all. This is what I wanted to say to the comrades present here.

In the last eight years the line, principles and policies our Party formulated at the Third Plenary Session of the Eleventh Central Committee have been smoothly implemented, our country has made notable progress and the living standards of the people have risen visibly. This reality cannot be negated by student disturbances. However, our strength is still limited. Until the end of the century we shall still be trying to shake off poverty. In 1980 our per capita GNP was only about $250, and today it is just a little over $400, a figure that puts us behind 100 countries in the world. By the end of the century, when we have become comparatively prosperous, the per capita GNP will have reached only $800 to 1,000. By then, we shall only have laid a fairly good foundation for the realization of our second goal. After another 30 or 50 years of effort, the Chinese people will have attained a medium standard of living. It seems to me that it should be possible for us to achieve both our first and second goals.

If we have been successful over the past eight years, it is chiefly because our policies were based on China's realities and because we relied on our own efforts. Our goals are realistic. Raising the people's standard of living is a long-term task. The mistakes we have made since the founding of the People's Republic were all due to overeagerness: disregarding China's realities, we set excessively high targets, with the result that progress was slowed. Building socialism is no easy job.

To achieve genuine political independence a country must first lift itself out of poverty. And to do that it must base its economic and foreign policies on its own conditions. It should not erect barriers to cut itself off from the world. China's experience shows that for a country to isolate itself from the outside is only to its own disadvantage.

If China is to develop, it must continue opening to the outside world and proceed with its reforms. These should also include reform of the political structure, which is in the realm of the superstructure. The policy of opening to the outside world is correct, and China has benefited greatly from it. If anything, we should open our doors even wider. And that's what we are going to do. Thanks to our great capacity of assimilation and to our correct policies, opening to the outside world will not affect the foundations of our socialist system. Educating our people in the Four Cardinal Principles will provide a fundamental guarantee of that.

WE MUST CONTINUE TO BUILD SOCIALISM AND ELIMINATE POVERTY*

April 26, 1987

Our two parties and countries were out of contact for quite some time. So far as our relations with the countries and parties of Eastern Europe are concerned, we are largely responsible for the problems that occurred. For a long time we didn't clearly understand the special situation these countries and parties were in. It was only after the downfall of the Gang of Four that we began to have a better grasp of these matters. Now we are clear about the events that took place in Poland and about the situation in your country. We all agreed to let bygones be bygones, and in recent years the dark clouds have been dissipated and our relations have been developing quite well. Visits have been exchanged between China and Czechoslovakia. Your visit here and the forthcoming visit of Comrade Zhao Ziyang to your country and of Comrade Gustav Husak to China will help to advance our relations to a new stage.[28] The past is behind us; let's look to the future.

Your country is a good many years ahead of ours in scientific and technological progress and in industrial development. China still lags behind in these areas, but not in all. Through co-operation we can each overcome our weak points by learning from the other's strong points. There are many

---

* Remarks to Premier Lubomir Strougal of the Czechoslovak Socialist Republic.

things we could learn from you. In the 1950s you gave us quite a lot of assistance. Along with other countries, you helped us to lay the foundation for our industrial development.

You have been very successful in your work, and it was no easy job for you to achieve what you have achieved. You have done better than we. When we say that we have done relatively good work, that only applies to the last eight years. We lost too much time, especially the decade of the "cultural revolution", when we created troubles for ourselves with disastrous results. But we have learned from experience.

The current principles and policies formulated at the Third Plenary Session of the Party's Eleventh Central Committee in December 1978 are the product of the lessons we learned from the "cultural revolution". The fundamental thing we have learned is that we must be clear about what socialism and communism are and about how to build socialism.

It seems that you and we share the same way of thinking, that our principles and policies regarding certain current problems and even some of the specific measures we have adopted are quite similar. Building socialism is our common goal, but the way of approaching it must be determined by the particular conditions in each country. I believe you can understand why we propose to build socialism with Chinese characteristics. Socialism in Czechoslovakia has to be tailored to Czechoslovak conditions, you can't just mechanically copy foreign models. For several decades we did that, but with poor results. Your country is different from Hungary and from Bulgaria too, and I think it is also different from the German Democratic Republic, although the latter is on a level of development close to yours.

In the past we stayed in a rut, engaging in construction

behind closed doors, and many years of hard work did not produce the desired results. It is true that we were making gradual progress, but on the whole our country remained at a standstill for a long time. We succeeded in developing certain things, such as the atomic bomb, the hydrogen bomb and even intercontinental ballistic missiles. But our people were still living in poverty. During the "cultural revolution", the Gang of Four raised the absurd slogan, "Better to be poor under socialism and communism than to be rich under capitalism." There is some justification for rejecting being rich under capitalism. But how can we advocate being poor under socialism and communism? It was that kind of thinking that brought China to a standstill. That situation forced us to re-examine the question. Our first conclusion was that we had to go on building socialism, and that to do that we had to eliminate poverty and backwardness, greatly develop the productive forces, and demonstrate the superiority of socialism over capitalism. To this end, we had to shift the focus of our work to the drive for modernization and make that our goal for the next few decades. Experience has taught us that we must no longer keep the country closed to the outside world and that we must bring the initiative of our people into full play. Hence our policies of opening up and reform. Our open policy has two aspects: domestic and international. The initiative of our people cannot be brought into full play without an open policy at home. The road we have taken is similar to yours. We began with the countryside, applying the open policy there, and we achieved results very quickly. In some places it took only one or two years to get rid of poverty. After accumulating the necessary experience in the countryside, we shifted the focus of reform to the cities. The urban reform has been under way for nearly three years, but much remains to be done. We also obtained quick results from the open policy internationally. But unlike your country, China lags many years behind in science and technology. We have far more problems to solve than you, especially the problem of our huge population, which already stands at 1.05 billion. This makes it very difficult for us to raise the people's income and to eliminate poverty and backwardness in a short time. In everything we do we must proceed from reality, seeing to it that targets are realistic and that enough time is allowed to fulfil them. I agree with what you said a moment ago, that the boat will eventually sink if we lose touch with reality and formulate our policies and project our development plans on the basis of wishful thinking. An example in this connection is the excessively high growth rate in the last quarter of 1984 and throughout 1985, which caused us some problems. That's why we needed some readjustment and contraction. But this had its good side too, because we learned from the experience.

On the whole, our goals are not too ambitious. We give ourselves 20 years—that is, from 1981 to the end of the century—to quadruple our GNP and achieve comparative prosperity, with an annual per capita GNP of $800 to $1,000. Then we will take that figure as a new starting point and try to quadruple it again, so as to reach a per capita GNP of $4,000 in another 50 years. What does this mean? It means that by the middle of the next century we hope to reach the level of the moderately developed countries. If we can achieve this goal, first, we will have accomplished a tremendous task; second, we will have made a real contribution to mankind; and third, we will have demonstrated more convincingly the superiority of the socialist system. As our principle of distribution is a socialist one, our per capita GNP of $4,000 will be different from the equivalent amount in the capitalist countries. For one thing, China has a huge population. If we assume that by the mid-21st century our population will have reached 1.5 billion and that we will have a per capita GNP of $4,000, then our total annual GNP will be $6,000 billion, and that will place China among the advanced countries of the world. By reaching that goal, we will not only blaze a new path for the people of the Third World, who represent three quarters of the world's population, but also —and this is even more important—we will demonstrate to mankind that socialism is the only solution and that it is superior to capitalism.

So, to build socialism it is necessary to develop the productive forces. Poverty is not socialism. We will go on building socialism, there's no doubt about that. But if it is to be superior to capitalism, it must enable us to eliminate poverty. We say that we are building socialism, but that doesn't mean that what we have achieved so far is up to the socialist standard. Not until the middle of the next century, when we have reached the level of the moderately developed countries, will we be able to claim that we have really built socialism and to declare convincingly that it is superior to capitalism. We are advancing towards that goal. In the course of building socialism and trying to modernize we have encountered some interference from the "Left". Since the Third Plenary Session of the Eleventh Central Committee of our Party, we have been concentrating on combating "Left" mistakes, because those are the ones we have made in the past. But there has also been interference from the Right. You have experienced this in your country too. What we mean by interference from the Right is the call for total westernization, which would lead not to a more advanced socialism but to capitalism. We have already coped with the recent student unrest and made some changes of personnel.

In short, the problems you and we are thinking about and

the roads you and we have taken are almost the same. We have been marching down this road for more than eight years. I think there's no question but that we will attain the goal we have set for the end of the century, although the next one, for the 50 years after that, will be harder to reach.

WE SHALL DRAW ON HISTORICAL EXPERIENCE AND GUARD AGAINST ERRONEOUS TENDENCIES*

April 30, 1987

The overall situation in China is good. Since the defeat of the Gang of Four and the convocation of the Third Plenary Session of the Party's Eleventh Central Committee in 1978, we have formulated a series of new principles and policies which have proved sound in practice. But this is only a beginning. We can consider that in the nine years since then we have taken the first step. Our goal for the first step is to reach, by 1990, a per capita GNP of $500, that is, double the 1980 figure of $250. The goal for the second step is, by the turn of the century, to reach a per capita GNP of $1,000. When we reach this goal, China will have shaken off poverty and achieved comparative prosperity. When the total GNP exceeds $1,000 billion, the country will be more powerful, although per capita GNP will still be very low. The goal we have set for the third step is the most important one—quadrupling the $1,000 billion figure of the year 2000 within another 30 to 50 years. That will mean that we have approached your present level—in other words, a medium standard of living. That target may not seem high, but it is a very ambitious goal for us, and it won't be easy to achieve.

---

* Remarks to Alfonso Guerra, Deputy General Secretary of the Spanish Workers' Socialist Party and Vice-Premier of Spain.

We are now confident that we can attain our first goal ahead of schedule, this year or next. That doesn't mean it will be easy to reach our second goal, but I think we can do it. Our third goal will be much harder to achieve than the first two. China is building socialism, and we have to demonstrate by our achievements that it is a superior system. Our experience over the last nine years or so shows that the road we have taken is the right one. But it is only after the third step that we will really be able to show the superiority of socialism over capitalism—that's something we can't prove at the moment. We will have to work hard for another 50 or 60 years. By then, people of my age will be gone, but I have no doubt that the younger generation will reach the third goal.

The image of China has really changed since the founding of the People's Republic. For more than a century since the Opium War China was subjected to humiliation, and the Chinese people were looked down upon. After 28 years of hard struggle under the leadership of the Communist Party, the people drove out the imperialist aggressors and overthrew the regime of Chiang Kai-shek. In 1949, when the People's Republic of China was founded, the Chinese people finally stood up. It is true that in the 38 years since then we have made a lot of mistakes. Our basic goal—to build socialism—is correct, but we are still trying to figure out what socialism is and how to build it. The primary task for socialism is to develop the productive forces. Our seizure of state power in 1949 liberated those forces as a whole, and the agrarian reform liberated the productive forces of the peasants, who constitute 80 per cent of China's population. So far so good. But we did a poor job of developing the productive forces. That was chiefly because we were in too much of a hurry and adopted "Left" policies, with the result that instead of accelerating the development of the productive forces, we hindered it. We began making "Left" mistakes in the political domain in 1957; in the economic domain those mistakes led to the Great Leap Forward of 1958, which resulted in much hardship for the people and enormous damage to production. From 1959 through 1961 we experienced tremendous difficulties—people didn't have enough to eat, not to mention anything else. In 1962 things began to look up, and production was gradually restored to its former level. But the "Left" thinking persisted. Then in 1966 came the "cultural revolution", which lasted a whole decade, a real disaster for China. During that period many veteran cadres suffered persecution, including me. I was labelled the "No. 2 Capitalist Roader" after Liu Shaoqi.[29] Liu was called "commander-in-chief of the bourgeois headquarters" and I "deputy commander-in-chief". Many strange things happened in those days. For instance, we were told that we should be content with poverty and backwardness and that it was better to be poor under socialism and communism than to be rich under capitalism. That was the sort of rubbish peddled by the Gang of Four. There is no such thing as socialism and communism with poverty. The ideal of Marxists is to realize communism. According to Marx, communist society is a society in which the principle of from each according to his ability, to each according to his needs is applied. What is the principle of to each according to his needs? How can we apply this principle without highly developed productive forces and vast material wealth? According to Marxism, communist society is a society in which there is overwhelming material abundance. Socialism is the first stage of communism and represents a long historical period. To build socialism we must develop the productive forces. Only if we constantly develop the productive forces can we finally achieve communism. The Gang of Four's absurd theory on socialism and communism led only to poverty and stagnation.

In the first couple of years after we had smashed the Gang of Four not all the "Left" mistakes that had been made were corrected. The years 1977 and 1978 were a period of hesitation in China. It was not until December 1978, when the Eleventh Central Committee convened its Third Plenary Session, that we began to make a serious analysis of our experience in the 30 years since the founding of new China. On the basis of that analysis we formulated a series of new policies, notably the policy of reform and the policy of opening up both internationally and domestically. We set forth a new basic line, which was to shift the focus of our work to economic construction, clearing away all obstacles and devoting all our energies to the drive for socialist modernization. To achieve modernization and to implement the reform and the open policy we need political stability and unity at home and a peaceful international environment. With this in mind, we have established a foreign policy which in essence comes down to opposition to hegemonism and preservation of world peace.

In the last eight or nine years our work has been successful, and the overall situation is good. That doesn't mean we haven't met with any obstacles. It's not so easy to rectify the "Left" thinking that has prevailed for several decades. "Left" thinking is our chief target because people have become used to it. There are not many in China who oppose reform. But in formulating and implementing specific policies, some people unintentionally reveal a yearning for the past. That's because old habits of thinking tend to reassert themselves. At the same time we have also encountered interference from the Right. Certain individuals, pretending to support the reform and the open policy, call for total westernization of China in an attempt to lead the country towards capitalism.

These people don't really support our policies; they are only trying vainly to change the nature of our society. If China were totally westernized and went capitalist, it would be impossible for us to modernize. The problem we have to solve is how to enable our one billion people to cast off poverty and become prosperous. If we adopted the capitalist system in China, probably less than 10 per cent of the population would be enriched, while over 90 per cent would remain in a permanent state of poverty. If that happened, the overwhelming majority of the people would rise up in revolution. China's modernization can be achieved only through socialism, not capitalism. There have been people who have tried to introduce capitalism into China and they have always failed. Generally speaking, we have changed the image of China, although in our efforts to build socialism we have made mistakes. There has been interference both from the Right and from the "Left", the "Left" interference being the more dangerous. That's because people have become accustomed to "Left" thinking, and it's not easy to change their ideology. As for some of our young people, they should be on guard against Right thinking, especially because they are not clear about what capitalism is and what socialism is. So we have to educate them about these things.

In our efforts to modernize, to introduce reform and to open to the outside world, we may encounter some dangers and difficulties. And we may make fresh mistakes, because China is such a big country and what we are doing is something that has never been done here before. Since China has its own characteristics, we can only run our affairs in accordance with the specific conditions in China. Of course, we can learn from the experience of others, but we must never copy everything. Since reform is a brand-new undertaking, mistakes are inevitable. We must not be afraid of making mistakes, and temporary setbacks must not make us abandon the reform and just mark time. We have to be daring, or we will never be able to modernize. But we also have to be cautious about introducing particular reforms and review our experience regularly. Minor errors are inevitable, but we should try to avoid major ones.

WE SHALL SPEED UP REFORM*

June 12, 1987

Since our two parties resumed contact we have had very good relations. It was Comrade Tito who visited China first and turned a new page in the history of relations between the two parties.[30] At that time our Party Chairman was Comrade Hua Guofeng. I met with Comrade Tito just as an old soldier. We had a cordial talk and agreed to forget the past and look to the future. This is the attitude we adopted when we resumed relations with other East European parties and countries: we take the present as a fresh starting point from which to develop friendly, co-operative relations. Of course, it's still worthwhile to analyse past experience. But I think the most important thing is that each party, whether it is big, small or medium, should respect the experience of the others and the choices they have made and refrain from criticizing the way they conduct their affairs. This should be our attitude not only towards parties in power but also towards those that are not in power. When we had talks with representatives of the Communist Parties of France and Italy, we expressed this view that we should respect their experience and their choices. If they have made mistakes, it is up to them to correct them. Likewise, they should take the same attitude towards us, allowing us to make mistakes and correct them. Every country and every party has its own experience, which

---

* Remarks to Stefan Korosec, member of the Presidium of the Central Committee of the League of Communists of Yugoslavia.

differs from that of the others in a thousand and one ways. We were opposed to the idea of a "patriarchal party", and our stand on that question has been proved correct. We were also opposed to the notion of a "centre". Unfortunately, we ourselves have been guilty of criticizing other parties. That experience taught us that a new type of relationship should be established between parties, and we therefore formulated this principle of mutual respect. I believe that if we abide by this principle, our friendship and co-operation will have a more solid and enduring foundation and that relations between the two parties and two countries will steadily improve.

China is now carrying out a reform. I am all in favour of that. There is no other solution for us. After years of practice it turned out that the old stuff didn't work. In the past we copied foreign models mechanically, which only hampered the development of our productive forces, induced ideological rigidity and kept people and grass-roots units from taking any initiative. We made some mistakes of our own as well, such as the Great Leap Forward and the "cultural revolution", which were our own inventions. I would say that since 1957 our major mistakes have been "Left" ones. The "cultural revolution" was an ultra-Left mistake. In fact, during the two decades from 1958 through 1978, China remained at a standstill. There was little economic growth and not much of a rise in the people's standard of living. How could we go on like that without introducing reforms? So in 1978, at the Third Plenary Session of the Eleventh Central Committee, we formulated a new basic political line: to give first priority to the drive for modernization and strive to develop the productive forces. In accordance with that line we drew up a series of new principles and policies, the major ones being reform and the open policy. By reform we mean something comprehensive, including reform of both the economic structure and the political structure and corresponding changes in all other areas. By the open policy we mean both opening to all other countries, irrespective of their social systems, and opening at home, which means invigorating the domestic economy.

We introduced reform and the open policy first in the economic field, beginning with the countryside. Why did we start there? Because that is where 80 per cent of China's population lives. An unstable situation in the countryside would lead to an unstable political situation throughout the country. If the peasants did not shake off poverty, it would mean that the majority of the people remained poor. So after the Third Plenary Session of the Eleventh Central Committee, we decided to carry out rural reform, giving more decision-making power to the peasants and the grass-roots units. By so doing we immediately brought their initiative into play. And by adopting a policy of diversifying agriculture, we substantially increased not only the output of grain but also the output of cash crops. The rural reform has achieved much faster results than we had anticipated. Frankly, before the reform the majority of the peasants were extremely poor, hardly able to afford enough food, clothing, shelter and transportation. Since the rural reform began they have shown their initiative. Bearing local conditions in mind, they have grown grain and cash crops in places suited to them. Since the peasants were given the power to decide for themselves what to produce, they have brought about a dramatic change in the rural areas. The reform was so successful that in many places it yielded tangible results within just one year. The peasants' income has increased substantially, sometimes even doubling or quadrupling. Of course, not everyone was in favour of reform at the outset. In the beginning two provinces took the lead: Sichuan—my home province—led by Comrade Zhao Ziyang, and Anhui, led by Comrade Wan Li, who is now our Acting Premier. We worked out the principles and policies of reform on the basis of the experience accumulated by these two provinces. For one or two years after we publicized these principles and policies, some provinces had misgivings about them and others didn't know what to think, but in the end they all followed suit. The Central Committee's policy was to wait for them to be convinced by facts.

Generally speaking, once the peasants' initiative was brought into play, the rural reform developed very quickly. Our greatest success—and it is one we had by no means anticipated—has been the emergence of a large number of enterprises run by villages and townships. They were like a new force that just came into being spontaneously. These enterprises engage in the most diverse endeavours, including both manufacturing and trade. The Central Committee takes no credit for this. The annual output value of these village and township enterprises has been increasing by more than 20 per cent every year for the last several years. In the first five months of this year their output value has been greater than in the corresponding period last year. This increase in village and township enterprises, particularly industrial enterprises, has provided jobs for 50 per cent of the surplus labour in the countryside. Instead of flocking into the cities, the surplus farm workers have been building up a new type of villages and townships. If the Central Committee made any contribution in this respect, it was only by laying down the correct policy of invigorating the domestic economy. The fact that this policy has had such a favourable result shows that we made a good decision. But this result was not anything that I or any of the other comrades had foreseen; it just came out of the blue. In short, the rural reform has produced rapid and noticeable results. Of course, that doesn't mean all the problems in the countryside have been solved.

The success of the reform in the countryside emboldened us to apply the experience we had gained from it to economic restructuring in the cities. That too has been very successful, although it is more complicated than rural reform.

In the meantime, the policy of opening China's doors to the outside world has produced the results we hoped for. We have implemented that policy in various ways, including setting up special economic zones and opening 14 coastal cities. Wherever the open policy has been implemented there have been notable results. First we established the Shenzhen Special Economic Zone. It was the leaders of Guangdong Province who came up with the proposal that special zones be established, and I agreed. But I said they should be called special *economic* zones, not special *political* zones, because we didn't want anything of that sort. We decided to set up three more special zones in addition to Shenzhen: Zhuhai and Shantou, both also in Guangdong Province, and Xiamen in Fujian Province. I visited Shenzhen a couple of years ago and found the economy flourishing there. The Shenzhen people asked me to write an inscription for them, and I wrote: "The development and experience of the Shenzhen Special Economic Zone prove the correctness of our policy of establishing such zones." At the time, a number of people of different political persuasions, from Hongkong journalists to Party members, were sceptical about that policy. They didn't think it would work. But the Shenzhen Special Economic Zone has achieved remarkable successes since it was established almost eight years ago. This zone is an entirely new thing, and it is not fair for the people who run it not to be allowed to make mistakes. If they have made mistakes, they were minor ones. The people in Shenzhen reviewed their experience and decided to shift the zone's economy from a domestic orientation to an external orientation, which meant that Shenzhen would become an industrial base and offer its products on the world market. It is only two or three years since then, and already the situation in Shenzhen has changed greatly. The comrades there told me that more than 50 per cent of their products were exported and that receipts and payments of foreign exchange were in balance. I am now in a position to say with certainty that our decision to establish special economic zones was a good one and has proved successful. All scepticism has vanished. Recently a comrade told me that the Xiamen Special Economic Zone is developing even faster than Shenzhen. When I visited Xiamen in 1984, there was only an airport surrounded by wasteland. Great changes have taken place there since then. Now we are preparing to make all of Hainan Island a special economic zone. Hainan Island, which is almost as big as Taiwan, has abundant natural resources, such as iron ore and oil, as well as rubber and other tropical and subtropical crops. When it is fully developed, the results should be extraordinary.

Our achievements in the last few years have proved the correctness of our policies of reform and of opening to the outside world. Although there are still problems in various fields, I don't think they'll be too hard to solve, if we go at it systematically. Therefore, we must not abandon these policies or even slow them down. One of the topics we have been discussing recently is whether we should speed up reform or slow it down. That's because reform and the open policy involve risks. Of course we have to be cautious, but that doesn't mean we should do nothing. Indeed, on the basis of our experience to date, the Central Committee has been considering to accelerate the reform and our opening to the outside world.

So much for reform of the economic structure.

Now a new question has been raised, reform of the political structure. This will be one of the main topics at the Thirteenth National Party Congress to be held next October. It's a complicated issue. Every measure taken in this connection will affect millions of people, mainly cadres, including the veterans. Generally speaking, reform of the political structure involves democratization, but what that means is not very clear. The democracy in capitalist societies is bourgeois democracy—in fact, it is the democracy of monopoly capitalists. It is no more than a system of multi-party elections and a balance of the three powers. Can we adopt this system? Ours is the system of the people's congresses and people's democracy under the leadership of the Communist Party. The greatest advantage of the socialist system is that when the central leadership makes a decision it is promptly implemented without interference from any other quarters. When we decided to reform the economic structure, the whole country responded; when we decided to establish the special economic zones, they were soon set up. We don't have to go through a lot of repetitive discussion and consultation, with one branch of government holding up another and decisions being made but not carried out. From this point of view, our system is very efficient. We should neither copy western democracy nor introduce the system of a balance of three powers. We should uphold socialist democracy, so as to retain the advantages of the socialist system. The efficiency I'm talking about is not efficiency of administration or economic management, but overall efficiency. We have superiority in this respect, and we should keep it. In terms of administration and economic management, the capitalist countries are more efficient than we in many respects. China is burdened with bureaucratism. Take our personnel system, for example. I think the socialist countries all have a problem of ageing cadres, so that leaders at all levels tend to be rigid in their thinking. But we think that to reform our political structure we can't copy the western system, the capitalist system. We socialist countries have to work out the content of the reform and take specific measures to implement it in the light of our own practice and our own conditions. The particular reform to be carried out in each socialist country is different too, and that is true of the East European countries. Since each has a different history, different experience and different current circumstances to confront, their reforms cannot be identical. Take China, for instance. We have a different point of view from yours on the question of reform. But we have in common the desire to retain our superiority and avoid the defects and evils that exist in capitalist societies.

What is the purpose of political restructuring? Its general purpose is to consolidate the socialist system, the leadership of the Party and the development of the productive forces under that system and that leadership. So far as China is concerned, the reform should also make it easier to implement the line, principles and policies laid down by the Party since the Third Plenary Session of its Eleventh Central Committee. To this end we have to do the following, I believe: (1) revitalize the Party, the administrative organs and the whole state apparatus, so that they are staffed with people whose thinking is not ossified and who can bring fresh ideas to bear on new problems; (2) increase efficiency; and (3) stimulate the initiative of the people and of the grassroots units in all fields of endeavour.

Revitalization. Here, the biggest problem is the need for younger cadres. In China the problem of ageing cadres with rigid ideas is more serious than it is in your country. For example, in our Central Committee the average age of members is higher than it is in the central committee of any other Communist Party in the world. The average age of the members of our Political Bureau, of its Standing Committee and of the Secretariat of the Central Committee is also quite high. There was no such problem when the People's Republic of China was founded. At that time the leaders were young. The problem of ageing leaders in the central organs didn't manifest itself until the Eleventh National Party Congress. There was an objective reason for this: a great many veterans who had been brought down during the "cultural revolution" were now rehabilitated and were resuming their posts at an advanced age. Take myself for example. I was only 52 when the Eighth National Party Congress was convened in 1956, but I was 72 when the "cultural revolution" ended in 1976. I was 73 when the Eleventh National Party Congress was held in 1977, and I will be 83 when the Thirteenth National Party Congress meets later this year. Some comrades are younger than I, but only by a few years; they are elderly too. This problem exists in leading organs at all levels and in all fields of endeavour. It is the outstanding problem in China. In general, old people tend to be conservative. They all have one thing in common: they consider problems only in the light of their personal experience. In today's world things are moving with unprecedented rapidity, especially in science and technology. There is an old saying in China, "Progress is made every day", and that's the way things are today. We must keep abreast of the times; that is the purpose of our reform. We must firmly carry out the policy of promoting younger cadres, but we must be cautious and proceed gradually. Of course, youth is not the only criterion for promoting cadres. They should have political integrity and professional competence, broad experience and familiarity with conditions, so as to form a reliable echelon of leaders of different years of age. We are bound to meet with obstacles and we will have to overcome them. It's going to take a lot of effort.

Increasing efficiency and eliminating bureaucratism. This includes, among other things, streamlining Party and government organs.

Stimulating people's initiative. The main idea is to delegate power to lower levels. The reason our rural reform has been so successful is that we gave the peasants more power to make decisions, and that stimulated their initiative. We are now applying this experience to all fields of work. When the people's initiative is aroused, that's the best manifestation of democracy.

These are the three objectives for our reform of the political structure. Democracy is an important means of carrying out our reform. But the question is how to put it into practice. Take general elections for instance. We run general elections at the lower levels, that is, for county and district posts, and indirect elections at the provincial and municipal and the central levels. China is such a huge country, with such an enormous population, so many nationalities and such varied conditions that it is not yet possible to hold direct elections at higher levels. Furthermore, the people's educational level is too low. So we have to stick to the system of people's congresses, in which democratic centralism is applied. The western two-chamber, multi-party system won't work in China. China also has a number of democratic parties, but they all accept leadership by the Communist Party. Ours is a system under which we make decisions after consultation with all the other parties. In this connection, even westerners agree that in a country as vast as China, if there were no central leadership many problems would be hard to solve, first of all, the problem of food. Our reform cannot depart from socialism, it cannot be accomplished without the leadership of the Communist Party. Socialism and Party leadership are interrelated; they cannot be separated from each other. Without the leadership of the Communist Party, there can be no building of socialism. We shall never again allow the kind of democracy we had during the "cultural revolution". Actually that was anarchy.

In short, so far as economic reform is concerned, the principles, policies and methods have been set. All we have to do now is to speed up their implementation. As for reform of the political structure, we are still discussing what its goals should be. We will work that out before the Thirteenth National Party Congress and launch the reform after that. It took three years for the rural economic reform to achieve good results, and it should take from three to five years for the urban economic reform to produce the visible results we expect. Reform of the political structure will be more complicated. In certain aspects, results can be obtained in from three to five years, but in certain others it may take ten.

NOTES

[1] This is the general objective of China's economic development for the two decades from 1981 to the end of this century. That is, while steadily improving economic performance, to quadruple the gross annual value of industrial and agricultural production—from 710 billion yuan in 1980 to about 2,800 billion yuan in 2000. p. 6

[2] In an interview with a correspondent from Xinhua News Agency on September 30, 1981, Ye Jianying, Chairman of the Standing Committee of the National People's Congress, elaborated on the nine principles concerning the return of Taiwan to the motherland for the peaceful reunification of China. These principles are as follows: p. 20

(1) In order to bring an end to the unfortunate separation of the Chinese nation as early as possible, we propose that talks be held between the Communist Party of China and the Kuomintang of China on a reciprocal basis so that the two parties can co-operate for the third time to accomplish the great cause of national reunification. The two sides may first send people to meet for an exhaustive exchange of views.

(2) It is the urgent desire of the people of all nationalities on both sides of the straits to communicate with each other, reunite with their families and relatives, develop trade and increase mutual understanding. We propose that the two sides make arrangements to facilitate the exchange of mail, trade, air and shipping services, family reunions and visits by relatives and tourists as well as academic, cultural and sports exchanges, and reach an agreement thereupon.

(3) After the country is reunified, Taiwan can enjoy a high degree of autonomy as a special administrative region and can retain its armed forces. The Central Government will not interfere with local affairs on Taiwan.

(4) Taiwan's current socio-economic system will remain unchanged, as will its way of life and its economic and cultural relations with foreign countries. There will be no encroachment on proprietary rights or on the lawful right of inheritance of private property, houses, land and enterprises, or on foreign investments.

(5) People in authority and representative personages of various circles in Taiwan may take up posts of leadership in national political bodies and participate in running the state.

(6) When Taiwan's local finances are in difficulty, the Central Government may offer subsidies as appropriate.

(7) For people of all nationalities and public figures of various circles in Taiwan who wish to settle on the mainland, we will guarantee that proper

arrangements will be made, that there will be no discrimination against them, and that they will have freedom of entry and exit.

(8) We hope that industrialists and businessmen in Taiwan will invest in the mainland and engage in economic undertakings there, and their legal rights, interests and profits will be guaranteed.

(9) The reunification of the motherland is the responsibility of all Chinese. We sincerely hope that people of all nationalities and public figures in all circles and all mass organizations in Taiwan will make proposals regarding affairs of state through various channels.

[3] In her opening speech to the First Session of the Sixth National Committee of the Chinese People's Political Consultative Conference on June 4, 1983, Deng Yingchao, executive Chairwoman of its Presidium, declared that "the peaceful reunification of the motherland is a common aspiration of the Chinese people of all nationalities and a glorious mission history has bequeathed to us". "We respect history and we respect reality," she said. "We give full consideration to the wishes of the people of all nationalities in Taiwan and to the circumstances the Taiwan authorities are in. We have in mind not only the immediate but also the long-term interest. After reunification of the motherland, the Communist Party and the Kuomintang will supervise, co-operate and coexist with each other for a long time to come. As a special administrative region, Taiwan may maintain a system different from that on the mainland, so that the two will complement and support each other; only if reunification is truly based on reality, can our country become strong, prosperous and dynamic. To support the reunification of the motherland means to love the country. On condition that the country is reunified, all problems can sooner or later be appropriately solved through consultation. It is our sincere hope that the people of all nationalities in Taiwan and our other compatriots in Hongkong and Macao and the Chinese nationals residing abroad, together with the people of various nationalities on the mainland, will continue to offer suggestions so as to contribute to peaceful reunification. But the Taiwan question is China's internal affair and no foreign interference in it will be tolerated." p. 20

[4] The "three types of people" are those who rose to prominence during the "cultural revolution" by following the Lin Biao and Jiang Qing counter-revolutionary cliques in "rebellion"; those who are still wedded to factionalism; and those who during the "cultural revolution" engaged in beating, smashing and looting. p. 25

[5] The northern warlords referred to here were the ones from several northern provinces, who were formed into a feudal clique by Yuan Shikai in the last years of the Qing Dynasty (1644-1911). After Yuan was appointed viceroy of Zhili Province and minister in charge of the northern coastal provinces in 1901, he gathered his followers around him and formed the clique. Shortly after the 1911 Revolution, he usurped the provisional presidency of the Republic and ushered in a period of rule by reactionary northern warlords. After his death in 1916, this network split into three separate cliques, backed by different imperialist powers. The regime of the northern warlords ended in 1928. p. 51

[6] This refers to Britain's war of aggression against China from 1840 to 1842. Beginning at the end of the 18th century, Britain smuggled great quantities of

opium into China. This traffic not only subjected the Chinese people to drug addiction but also represented a massive drain on China's silver reserves. At the end of 1838 the Qing government sent Lin Zexu as an imperial commissioner to Guangzhou to put a stop to opium-smoking and the opium trade. In June the following year Lin ordered the public burning of more than 1.15 million kilogrammes of opium confiscated from British and American merchants engaged in illegal activities. In 1840, under the pretext of protecting its trade with China, Britain launched a war of aggression against China. The Qing government vacillated and made compromises during the war. Only the people and some of the Chinese troops rose in resistance. The British troops harassed and invaded the coastal areas of Guangdong, Fujian and Zhejiang provinces and went on to capture Wusong and places along the Changjiang River, posing a direct threat to Nanjing. In August 1842 the Qing government was forced to sign the humiliating "Treaty of Nanjing". From then on China was reduced to a semi-colonial and semi-feudal society. p. 53

[7] In May 1984 the Chinese government further decided to open 14 coastal cities: Tianjin, Shanghai, Dalian, Qinhuangdao, Yantai, Qingdao, Lianyungang, Nantong, Ningbo, Wenzhou, Fuzhou, Guangzhou, Zhanjiang and Beihai. p. 57

[8] Hu Yaobang, born in 1915 in Liuyang County, Hunan Province, is now a member of the Standing Committee of the Political Bureau of the Central Committee. At the time in question he was General Secretary of the Central Committee. p. 72

[9] Zhao Ziyang, born in 1919 in Huaxian County, Henan Province, is a member of the Standing Committee of the Political Bureau of the Central Committee and Premier of the State Council. In January 1987 hc was elected Acting General Secretary of the Central Committee. p. 72

[10] Zheng He (1371-1435) was an outstanding Chinese navigator in the Ming Dynasty. For 28 years starting in 1405, he was continually sent with a fleet under his command to sail the Indian Ocean. On his voyages he visited more than 30 countries, going as far as the east coast of Africa and the mouth of the Red Sea. He helped to promote economic and cultural exchanges between China and other countries in Asia and Africa. p. 79

[11] Kang Xi was the title given to the reign of Emperor Sheng Zu (1662-1722) of the Qing Dynasty. Qian Long was the title given to the reign of Emperor Gao Zong (1736-95) of the same dynasty. p. 79

[12] The Five Principles of Peaceful Coexistence are: mutual respect for sovereignty and territorial integrity, mutual non-aggression, non-interference in each other's internal affairs, equality and mutual benefit, and peaceful coexistence. p. 87

[13] Yu Qiuli, born in 1914 in Ji'an County, Jiangxi Province, is a member of the Political Bureau of the Central Committee and Director of the General Political Department of the People's Liberation Army. p. 92

[14] The "five things to emphasize" are: behaviour, civility, hygiene, discipline and morals. The "four things to beautify" are: thoughts, words, deeds and the environment. And the "three things to love" are: the motherland, socialism and the Communist Party. p. 101

[15] In June 1950 the Central People's Government promulgated the Agrarian Reform Law and a few months later began to launch the agrarian reform movement in the newly liberated areas. By winter 1952 the reform had been basically completed throughout the country, except in Taiwan Province and some minority nationality areas. About 300 million peasants who had a little land or no land at all received some 700 million *mu* (one *mu* is 1/15 hectare) of land, together with other means of production. p. 105

[16] After the completion of the agrarian reform, the Communist Party called on the peasants to organize first into temporary or year-round mutual-aid teams and later into co-operatives. In the lower-stage agricultural producers' co-operatives land was pooled as shares, management was unified and incomes were distributed according to land shares and labour input. In the higher-stage co-operatives ownership of land was turned over to the collective and incomes were distributed according to work done. By the end of 1956, 96.3 per cent of the peasant households throughout China had been brought into producers' co-operatives. Thus the socialist transformation of individual farming was basically complete. p. 105

[17] The socialist transformation of capitalist industry and commerce was begun immediately after the founding of the People's Republic in 1949 and was basically completed in 1956. Operating on the Marxist-Leninist theory that under certain circumstances the proletariat can adopt a policy of redemption with regard to the bourgeoisie, the Communist Party followed a policy of utilizing, restricting and transforming capitalist industry and commerce as was suited to the nature of the Chinese national bourgeoisie. A whole series of transitional forms of state capitalism were introduced, including the placing of state orders with private enterprises for the processing of materials or the manufacture of goods, state monopoly of the purchase and marketing of the products of private enterprises, the marketing of products of state-owned enterprises by private shops, and joint state-private ownership of individual enterprises or of all enterprises in a single trade. Through this process, capitalist industry and commerce were integrated into the socialist public economy. p. 105

[18] The "Great Leap Forward" was a mass movement initiated in 1958 without much consideration. In August of that year, at an enlarged meeting of the Political Bureau of the Central Committee, it was decided that in 1958 the output of steel should be 10.7 million tons, double the output in 1957, and that people's communes should be established throughout the countryside. The movement for steelmaking and for the establishment of rural people's communes soon swept the country. As a result, "Left" errors—the setting of unrealistic targets, the issuing of arbitrary orders, exaggerated claims of achievement and the launching of a drive for communization—spread unchecked. All this disrupted normal economic development, wasted enormous human and material resources, distorted the balance of the economy and adversely affected the daily life of the people. The "Great Leap Forward" movement was not stopped until the winter of 1960. p. 105

[19] In April 1957 the Central Committee launched a Party-wide rectification movement against bureaucratism, sectarianism and subjectivism. Taking advantage of this, a handful of bourgeois Rightists attacked the Party and the newly installed socialist system in an attempt to supplant Communist Party leadership. In June the

Central Committee issued a directive calling for beating back their attack. This was necessary. But a serious mistake was made in enlarging the scope of the struggle to include many persons who were not, in fact, Rightists. In 1978 the Central Committee decided to re-examine the cases of those who had been designated as Rightists and to exonerate those who were found to have been wrongly labelled as such. p. 120

[20] Liu Qingshan was at one time Secretary of the Tianjin Prefectual Party Committee and then Deputy Secretary of the Shijiazhuang Municipal Party Committee. Zhang Zishan became Secretary of the Tianjin Prefectural Party Committee after Liu had left. Corrupted by bourgeois ideas, they engaged in embezzlement on a large scale and were sentenced to death in 1952. p. 138

[21] Fang Lizhi, born in 1936 in Hangzhou, Zhejiang Province, was Vice-President of the Chinese University of Science and Technology in Hefei. Because he advocated bourgeois liberalization, in opposition to the Four Cardinal Principles, it was decided that he was no longer qualified for Party membership, and on January 17, 1987 he was expelled from the Party. He is now a research fellow at the Beijing Observatory under the Chinese Academy of Sciences. p. 162

[22] Wang Ruowang, born in 1917 in Wujin, Jiangsu Province, is a council member of the Shanghai Writers' Association and of the Chinese Writers' Association. Because he preached bourgeois liberalization and opposed the Four Cardinal Principles, it was decided that he was no longer qualified for Party membership, and on January 13, 1987 he was expelled from the Party. p. 162

[23] Zhou Gucheng, born in 1898 in Yiyang, Hunan Province, is a professor of history at Fudan University in Shanghai, Chairman of the Central Committee of the Chinese Peasants' and Workers' Democratic Party and Vice-Chairman of the Standing Committee of the National People's Congress. p. 164

[24] Fei Xiaotong, born in 1910 in Wujiang, Jiangsu Province, is a professor of sociology at Beijing University and at the Central Institute for Nationalities, Chairman of the Central Committee of the China Democratic League and Vice-Chairman of the National Committee of the Chinese People's Political Consultative Conference. p. 164

[25] Qian Weichang, born in 1912 in Wuxi, Jiangsu Province, is President of Shanghai Polytechnic University, Vice-Chairman of the Central Committee of the China Democratic League and Vice-Chairman of the National Committee of the CPPCC. p. 164

[26] Liu Binyan, born in 1925 in Changchun, Jilin Province, is a journalist on the staff of *Renmin Ribao* (*People's Daily*) and Vice-Chairman of the Chinese Writers' Association. Because he advocated bourgeois liberalization and opposed the Four Cardinal Principles, he was no longer qualified for Party membership and was expelled from the Party on January 23, 1987. p. 164

[27] Li Ruihuan, born in 1934 in Baodi, Tianjin, is Deputy Secretary of the Tianjin Municipal Party Committee and Mayor of Tianjin. p. 166

[28] Gustav Husak, born in 1913, is General Secretary of the Central Committee of the Communist Party of Czechoslovakia and President of the Czechoslovak Socialist Republic. p. 174

[29] Liu Shaoqi (1898-1969), a native of Ningxiang, Hunan Province, was then Vice-Chairman of the Central Committee and Chairman of the People's Republic of China. When the "cultural revolution" started in 1966, he was wrongly criticized and accused by the counter-revolutionary cliques of Lin Biao and Jiang Qing of being a "capitalist roader" and a renegade. He suffered physical persecution at their hands and died in 1969. In 1980 the Central Committee adopted a resolution clearing his name. p. 182

[30] Josip Broz Tito (1892-1980) was then Chairman of the League of Communists of Yugoslavia and President of the Socialist Federal Republic of Yugoslavia. He visited China from August 30 to September 8, 1977. p. 186

论当代中国基本问题

邓小平

*

外文出版社出版

（中国北京百万庄路24号）

外文印刷厂印刷

中国国际图书贸易总公司

（中国国际书店）发行

北京399信箱

1987年（大32开）英第一版

17050－3026

17050－3027

ISBN 7－119－00344－5/D·21

ISBN 7－119－00345－3/D·22

00845（精）

00735（平）

3－E－2229